BACK TO PARADISE

BACK *to* PARADISE

BILLY McNEILL

with

ALEX CAMERON

MAINSTREAM
PUBLISHING

First published in Great Britain in 1988 by
MAINSTREAM PUBLISHING COMPANY (EDINBURGH) LTD
7 Albany Street
Edinburgh EH1 3UG

British Library Cataloguing in Publication Data

McNeill, Billy
    Back to paradise.
    1. Scotland. Association football. McNeill, Billy
    I. Title   II. Cameron, Alex
    796.334′092′4

    ISBN 1-85158-187-1
    ISBN 1-85158-188-X Pbk

Typeset in 11 on 13 point Times by Pulse Origination, Edinburgh.
Printed in Great Britain by Billings and Son Ltd, Worcester.

In appreciation of Liz's 25 years of patience and support.

CONTENTS

Foreword **9**

Chapter One: *The Second Time Around* **11**

Chapter Two: *In The Beginning* **40**

Chapter Three: *The Big Man* **52**

Chapter Four: *The Lisbon Lions* **62**

Chapter Five: *My Big Cash Crash* **74**

Chapter Six: *Scottish Football Revolution* **81**

Chapter Seven: *Moving In Management* **97**

Chapter Eight: *South Of The Border* **120**

Chapter Nine: *The Media And Me* **140**

Chapter Ten: *Whistling While They Work* **148**

Chapter Eleven: *The International Scene* **156**

Chapter Twelve: *Games And Goals To Remember* **165**

Chapter Thirteen: *Why "King" Kenny Is Such A Marvel* . **182**

Chapter Fourteen: *My Élite Elevens* **193**

Chapter Fifteen: *The Way Ahead For Celtic* **199**

Appendices: **207**

Foreword

IT IS an astonishing fact that only once previously has a manager of Celtic written a book and that was Willie Maley exactly 50 years ago. Certainly that book, which was to coincide with the club's golden jubilee, was done in the form of a history of the club and it remains to this day a much cherished possession of many Celtic fans, albeit having been handed down from generation to generation.

This book by Billy McNeill is much more an autobiographical work and by coincidence is also being published in a very important year in the history of Celtic Football Club.

The book starts with Billy's quite unexpected return to Celtic Park in 1987 which for once was one of those sensational stories that no member of the media got the slightest hint of in advance.

He speaks with candour on the circumstances surrounding his departure in contentious circumstances from Celtic Park in 1983, when it would have been easier to skirt around that quite traumatic episode in the club's history. In truth, as a member of the board at that time, I cannot allow the chairman of that period, Desmond White, to be saddled with most of the blame for that acrimonious parting of the ways. If there were wrongs, there were wrongs on both sides. Billy is man enough to admit to his own impetuous shortcomings. If there were wrongs on the side of the board they must be shared by all of the directors.

In many ways I found the chapter "In the Beginning" the most interesting, and I think it may prove to be particularly illuminating to younger readers who are not so aware of how much the monetary side of the game has changed in 30 years. One aspect that remains unchanged, however, is the Celtic fever which has affected and continues to affect youngsters on their first visit to Celtic Park — "Paradise" — over a period of 100 years.

I can honestly say that as I read through the book, from the chapter on the late Jock Stein, through the era of the Lisbon Lions and to the concluding chapter on the way ahead for Celtic, I was thoroughly engrossed.

Football books seem to abound nowadays and very often there is a sameness and repetitiveness to be found in their composition. This book does not fall into that category at all and I am absolutely certain that, having read it, the reader will be in total agreement with my opinion.

John C McGinn
Chairman, Celtic FC

Chapter One

The Second Time Around

THE silence was broken by the shrill but insistent ringing of the telephone. I was tempted not to answer because at the time my spirits were at zero. Just sacked very publicly by Aston Villa and now back in Glasgow on a whirlwind visit, I wondered what I should, or could, do next to earn a living. It was the lowest point in my life. I had taken my place in the dole queue at Altrincham. It was the first time I had "signed on" at the Labour Exchange since leaving school in 1957.

Answering that telephone call began a chain of moves over the next three days which would dramatically change my life. Jack McGinn, the Celtic chairman, was at the other end and asked briefly if he could see me for a chat. He didn't say why and I didn't ask. But I could hope, couldn't I?

I had come to Scotland from Manchester to attend a function in the Normandy Hotel at Renfrew run by the registered Celtic supporters' clubs to mark the 20th anniversary of Celtic winning the European Cup in Lisbon. All the Lions were present and were given a great reception. As captain, I had to make a short speech and, at the end of it, I was treated to a standing ovation. The fans seemed to like what I had to say and, I admit, I had given my speech a good deal of careful thought beforehand. This may have been the start of my return to Paradise — I have never found out — but the most welcome invitation I've ever had came only two days after that Sunday night appearance.

On the Monday, I attended the Manager of the Year lunch at the MacDonald Hotel in Giffnock and saw Jim McLean, of Dundee United, being presented with the trophy. I didn't dream that a year

11

later he would hand it to me after Celtic's double in the League Championship and Scottish Cup.

On the following day I planned to return to Manchester and give some thought to going back into the pub or hotel business. I was the guest in Glasgow of my friends Mike and Pat Jackson and they persuaded me to stay on for a few days, although I hadn't come prepared for a longer visit. I had only one thing left to do and that was to take part in a recording session at Radio Clyde about the Lisbon Lions. So when Jack McGinn contacted me I told him this and he hit on the idea of us meeting in the car park at Clydebank, which wasn't too far from his home in Dumbarton. Nobody would ever suspect that two men sitting in a car so close to a radio station would be discussing something which would soon be banner headlines.

Without beating about the bush Jack immediately asked me if I would like to return to Celtic as manager. I had hoped this was his reason for wanting to talk to me. But I couldn't be sure. The way my luck had gone in that year there was no sense in anticipating anything. He then began to detail what Celtic would offer me. I replied: "Jack, I'm not really interested in the details. You've asked me a question and the answer is 'Yes'."

The next problem was that I had to meet the rest of the board and it had to be done secretly the next day. In a city like Glasgow nothing in football can be kept quiet for long. I suggested we assemble at the Jackson home in the Queen's Park district of Glasgow. Mike and Pat were at work so this wouldn't cause them any bother. The meeting went off just fine.

The directors then had to face a situation with Davie Hay in which they had to say: "Sorry . . . but we have to make a change." The chairman had to speak to Davie but the whole board were quite genuinely distressed about having to sack a manager. For my part, I had feelings for Davie as well. The easy thing was for me to say thanks, and, yes, I'll take the job. But I had just been booted myself so I knew exactly how Davie would be feeling. He had my sympathy but there was nothing more I could do.

When I left the manager's job at Celtic Park in the first place and later learned that Davie Hay was succeeding me I phoned to wish him good luck. And when I moved back I called him at his home to say I was sad about what had happened to him. He understood my

Jack McGinn, Chairman of Celtic.

position perfectly. I also told him that if he wanted to come to the Park all he had to do was phone me and I would be happy to make sure he was looked after.

I liked Davie as a person. I appreciated his abilities as a player and a team-mate. I never had any argument with him. It's not the easiest thing in the world to accept that you're out of a job. But I also realised the board didn't find it straightforward making the change. The fact that Davie is such a likeable man added to their discomfort. It cast my mind back to me driving to Manchester to take over City and knowing that Davie had to be persuaded to replace me. Davie actually said that he had been "talked into" taking the job as Celtic manager. This contrasted with my feelings. I was desperate to get back, having always regarded the Celtic job as mine. When I was offered it again I couldn't say no.

In truth, I could never see myself returning to Celtic but I always hoped that it would happen. Lots of friends said I would eventually get the job again but I thought it was wishful thinking. When it did happen it was so quick it was scarcely believable that my dream had come true. A lot of fans may have been confused by the fact that Davie was allowed to spend £500,000 on Mick McCarthy so soon before parting with the club. I never questioned the reasoning behind the move. I was simply happy at the way it turned out for me.

I am eternally grateful to the Celtic board for taking me back. It was easy for them to offer the job but the decision leading up to it was momentous as far as I was concerned. I wouldn't have said "Yes" to just any job. It was necessary to be sure I could tackle it wholeheartedly. Being manager of Celtic is the pinnacle as far as I'm concerned. Hopefully, this is me at Parkhead for the rest of my working life. Especially as I now feel so much better qualified to be the manager. My firm intention is to be around as long as Celtic want me.

Many may still think my move was well planned but, believe me, it wasn't so. My return was exactly as I have said. And I believe the Celtic board would have been as surprised as me had somebody suggested the change to them only a week before. All sides were taken by surprise. I was the initial winner but I hope all connected with the club will agree that Celtic had a victory as well.

Had I not returned to Parkhead this would have been the most difficult year of my life. Not to be a part of the club's centenary would have been a major blow. I remember a couple of years before, when Celtic played at Nottingham Forest, I felt very peculiar to be merely watching as manager of Manchester City. It was difficult because I had to stay away from players and officials, although I did go to the dressing-room and wish the lads good luck.

It took some time, when I went to Maine Road at first, to remember that it was City fixtures I had to look at and not Celtic's. What delighted me in my come-back to Celtic was that my daughters and son, Martyn, also enjoyed the thrill of their dad being with such a successful club. Martyn, particularly, has been able to share my love of Celtic and this has pleased me incredibly.

Most of us want to do well to ensure that our families are given the benefit of what has been achieved and hopefully they grow up that little bit better off. Equally, the closeness and support of a family is important and that's something in which I have been very fortunate. When I look back I've given them a goodly share of anguish but the way they have accepted situations without being demonstrative about it has been heartening. Susan, Carol and Libby, the older girls, Paula who is much younger and Martyn have all been marvellous. I have tried to keep them out of the prying eye of publicity and they clearly like the anonynimity. In fact, they will be blazing when they read this but I feel I have to say it. The picture of them, specially taken for this book, was allowed only after a great deal of persuasion by their Mum. Everyone needs their family, and especially at difficult times when they stand up and support you. They can understand inner feelings. I've had these moments and their support and loyalty — led, of course, by Liz, my wife — have never been in doubt.

Men like to think they are the boss in the home but all of us know that the greater influence is the woman behind the man. I have been very, very fortunate in this respect as well. Ours has been a very happy marriage although I must admit that I used to take too many problems home. If we lost a game I could be difficult to live with. However, experience in the job has taught me this is pointless. It is important to do a job as well as possible but there's no sense in taking worries home because this won't solve anything.

When I arrived for a Press Conference at my Paradise I realised right away the place had changed. Nothing material at that stage,

This is my family in a special picture taken by Eric Craig just before Liz and I celebrated our silver wedding. That's Carol, Paula, Susan and Libby at the back with Martyn between his Mum and Dad.

but I felt it wasn't buzzing. I always believe that stadiums talk. Parkhead was saying nothing to me. It was dull, dreary and depressing. Part of the reason for this may have been the fact that a manager had just departed. There were also problems with players who were making noises about their contracts. There was an air of despondency.

Later I spent hours and hours talking to Tommy Craig, John Kelman and Neilly Mochan trying to get to grips with the problems. That was a long drawn-out period. Tommy, of course, was already with Celtic when I joined. He was worried about his position as assistant manager. However, I had known him for a long time: not particularly closely, but I was aware of his reputation as a skilful player. I had met him in England and found

16

The Happy Lads . . . Tommy Craig and I — very quickly we found there was a rapport between us.

him easy to talk to. One of the first things I did was to ring him to explain I was the manager. I arranged a chat and it was quickly apparent that Tommy would like to have been a player at Parkhead but never had the opportunity. Now he was delighted to be involved on the staff.

Tommy was disillusioned. The Celtic that he had encountered in a short spell under Davie Hay was not the one he had visualised. I told him that, because of the speed of my switch back, I had not been able to consider what changes I should make at the club. However, I informed Tommy that if we could quickly develop an understanding I saw no problems about him staying and working with me. Very quickly we found there was a rapport between us and, looking back, I don't think I've enjoyed working with anybody more than Tommy.

Although we're different people I see an awful lot of the younger

17

McNeill in him. This pleases me. I respect his ability and I think he has a great future in the game. By the time we started pre-season training we were on each other's wavelength and began planning together. When we got to Sweden for a series of trial matches we knew we had a good relationship.

It was in Sweden that the foundations for our double-winning performance in the club's centenary year were laid. The Celtic I had left weren't great, but they were organised and professional. The team I inherited had a lot of players who seemed unaware of basic team principles so we had to work on discipline and relationships. By this I mean we had to get an understanding between the back players, the midfield and the front men. We laboured very hard on this.

The games gave us a good basis. I was far from happy but we had made a start and were going the right way. I knew the first season back was very important for me. It was necessary to achieve something. I'm not saying winning the League, but it was important to demonstrate to everyone that Celtic were on the way up. I also needed to reinforce my confidence. I had taken a hard knock at Villa and I needed to show that I had recovered from it.

What heartened me more than anything was the response from the Celtic fans. I was swamped with letters and that gives anybody a lift. However, I decided that I wasn't going to be influenced — even by those super supporters. I had to do it my way. I knew that patience was essential. I was prepared to wait for the players I wanted.

I thought our best hope was to finish high enough in the League to qualify for the UEFA Cup. I never expected the team to win anything. We were well short. It would have been easy to rush into signings but I wasn't prepared to do that. Moves were being made all over the place, but I couldn't get the players I wanted. Not immediately, that is.

I wanted Joe Miller and Frank McAvennie quickly. My first signing might have been McAvennie but West Ham manager John Lyall lobbed my inquiry out of court. The fans reacted and told us what they wanted. I would never ignore the club's supporters but I felt that if I gave in it would be taking the easy way out. The fans would have been the manager and not me. Sometimes decisions have to be taken that are not particularly popular but that's what

8 August 1987: Andy Walker scores in Celtic's opening game against Morton. Davie Wyllie is the diving keeper.

management is about. I must dictate dressing-room policy. I have to oversee all playing matters on behalf of the club.

So few things went wrong in my first season that I suppose some people were joking that we had walked on water. It would be easy to say that my decisions have been the reason for the club's success but, being honest, luck also played a part. I know that at times we make our own luck, but in the first quarter of the season, for instance, we were fortunate to escape bad injuries.

When I first met the players I laid down a code of discipline which I believed to be sensible and adult. I like to set standards which the players will accept and then make sure they maintain them. I ban jeans, for instance. Not because I think players should never wear them. It's simply that jeans are casual and I believe that those wearing them become similarly minded. Footballers must be positive and also look the part. I don't want fans saying Celtic players are sloppy and lazy. It may seem minor, but discipline is founded on the simple things.

I wouldn't mind if players appeared every day in track suits. We are sporting people and modern track suits look extremely with-it. If any one of my players turned up wearing jeans you can bet I wouldn't be the first to tell them. The others would do it before me. Dress was only the start of my standard-setting. I told the players they would train at ten o'clock and this meant that at 10.01 they were a minute late. They could wait for me but I would never wait for them. Training had been at ten-thirty before my arrival but I felt this was 30 minutes wasted. Normally I check in at nine, change and do things like handling mail and talking to the Press before going to training. If I turn up after ten it's because I've been handling club business.

Our birthday season began abysmally and I'm sure even our most ardent fans thought we were going to have a really bad time. Arsenal beat us 5-1 in a friendly. Charlie Nicholas scored the first goal, which added to the annoyance. The easy thing would have been to dismiss the match as meaningless. I realised the lads were lacking in self-confidence. If I had hung my head at that stage, demonstrated the same lack of belief, it could have been a black season. Instead, I lectured the players about the way defeats such as this can happen in football. What we had to do was work even harder. I recalled Frank McClintock telling me Arsenal had been slammed during the year they won the double.

The League season began for us against Morton. It so happened that in my previous spell with Celtic the big kick-off had also been at Cappielow so I knew only too well how hard it could be. A promoted team on their own ground are always hard openers. I needn't have worried. The lads were brilliant. Mark McGhee and Billy Stark scored and Andy Walker got two in the second half to give us a 4-0 start. So all of a sudden McGhee, who tends to get the wrath of the fans more than most, had put himself into favour and Stark, whom some doubted as a Celtic player, had also made his mark. On top of this Walker, another new signing, had banged in two so we were off to a great start.

The first quarter of our League programme was a hard-working effort. We were determined and controlled. It was effective but I realised Celtic fans, although understanding the need for patience, also like us to play with flair. We had worked very hard on our passing and it was great against Morton. We also practised closing-down opponents and in the early games it came off for us. There is a story about Gary Player chipping out of a bunker and a spectator telling him his shot was a fluke, to which Gary is said to have responded: "It's a funny thing . . . the harder I practise the luckier I get!" This is true of football and everything else in life. The Celtic staff, at every level, certainly worked for the coveted double.

In the early games we also beat Hearts and Motherwell at Celtic Park. The 1-0 result against Hearts was particularly pleasing because our record hadn't been good against them. They were hard-fought matches in which Celtic showed that they would persevere to the last kick. Mark McGhee got the goal against Hearts while Mark, Andy Walker (2) and Stark got the four in the 4-1 defeat of Tommy McLean's team. We lost to Dunfermline and I felt this was one we should have won. The Fifers' goalie had a blinder and we went down 2-1. Our points tallies for each quarter were 16, 18, 19 and 19. So we finished with a Premier League record points tally of 72 in which we lost only three games to Dunfermline (away), Dundee United (home) and Hearts (away). The previous lowest number of defeats had been four in a season by Aberdeen. This was tremendous for us.

All I had wanted was a start that kept us in touch. The players obliged. I hoped, of course, to be able to go into the market.

Significant things began to happen. Frank McAvennie was signed but he wasn't the fit guy who had so recently been turning defenders over. We had to work to get him back to this standard. Then we had another team top-up with the introduction of Joe Miller from Aberdeen. On top of this Paul McStay and Roy Aitken signed long-term contracts. All of a sudden players showed belief in the club and, I hoped, in me as manager.

Slowly things began to fall into place. The first of our meetings with Rangers was a 1-0 victory and, of course, we were to take seven of the eight League points from matches with the Ibrox club — pure delight for our fans.

We lost 1-0 to a great Jim Bett goal in the Skol Cup quarter-final at Aberdeen. We were the better side and should have won, which made it more annoying. We were going through a bad patch then and it was worrying. A goalless draw with Dundee United at Tannadice followed and then we recovered to beat Falkirk with a goal by Tommy Burns. We also beat Borussia Dortmund 2-1 in the UEFA Cup first round in which Murdo MacLeod made his initial appearance at Parkhead after signing for the West German club in the close season. After that we drew 2-2 with Aberdeen at Celtic Park, but we chucked away a two-goal lead set up for us by Andy Walker and Derek Whyte. This was terrible. But for Jim Leighton's brilliance — what a save he had to prevent us going to 3-0 — Celtic would have won easily. Anyway, we conceded a last-minute goal to the Dons, scored by none other than Joe Miller.

People began to say that Celtic couldn't last the pace and generally dismissed us from the running in the championship. We were called a first half team, something we later took great pleasure disproving. Meantime, it wasn't good for our morale — or our egos.

Next we beat St Mirren with a Derek Whyte goal, but it was a drab and dismal game of which we weren't proud. The return match with Borussia presented us with problems. Mark McGhee had been injured and we were left with one genuine striker, Andy Walker. We were so inadequate it was unbelievable. I looked through the team and decided that I had to gamble with Mick McCarthy. I brought him in to play sweeper with Anton Rogan on the left and Chris Morris at right-back. Allen McKnight was in goal. McCarthy teamed with Derek Whyte and Roy Aitken in the

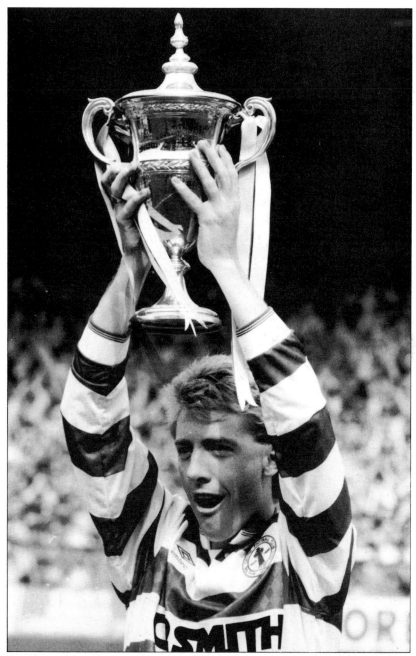

Significant things began to happen — Frank McAvennie was signed. Not too long afterwards he was holding the Scottish Cup.

middle. I looked at our bench and it underlined how short we were. Yet we created four or five chances in the match which could have made it a different result entirely. The two goals we lost were certainly preventable.

We returned to meet Hibs at Parkhead and gave them the runaround in the first half. But we struggled badly afterwards and the result was 1-1. We had the same result in the following week at Dundee after fighting back when we lost a goal just on half-time. Our next match marked McAvennie's debut and we won 3-1 against Morton. Frank scored the second goal. We started brilliantly but finished shockingly. I thought we should have won by five or six and I wasn't too pleased.

Our next game, against Rangers at Ibrox, fell into the same category. This was the infamous match in which referee Jim Duncan, of Gorebridge, ordered off McAvennie, the Rangers goalie Chris Woods and central defender Terry Butcher. It was a sad day for football because, of course, it led to court proceedings which involved these three players, plus Graham Roberts. Frank was found "not guilty", Roberts was "not proven" but Woods was fined £500 and Butcher £250. The charges related to incitement to cause a breach of the peace.

I make no comment on these individual cases. But the general principle of police becoming involved in field discipline has opened a door which is very dangerous for sport generally. Referees must be the sole arbiters of what happens during play. They alone should have the right to say whether a player is sent off, booked or merely warned. Once outside influences enter into football then the whole game is wrong. Players sent off are immediately punished by the very act of walking to the dressing-room. They then have to meet their manager and he disciplines them as well — as I did in McAvennie's case.

Players are next dealt with by the SFA who impose an automatic ban for one or more games. It is unfair for still another authority, albeit the law of the land, to step in with additional sanctions. It is also very easy for the uncommitted to watch a TV video — away from the emotions and the atmosphere — and say this or that shouldn't have happened. Policing of football is, of course, necessary and we tell players that they should at all times exercise the utmost restraint.

Neither the emotion nor the physical contact can be removed from football. Things will inevitably happen on the spur of the moment. When players lose their cool it isn't premeditated. Nor are the passions of play intended to incite trouble on the terracings or in the stands. So when people outside the game pass judgments there is a serious risk that harm will be done to the whole structure. I have never accepted that incidents on the pitch cause crowd trouble. In fact, they may well keep the fans entertained and restrained. I can't think of one occasion in my career when a field incident could unmistakably have been blamed for trouble among spectators. There are adequate controls within the game and when these are removed or subordinated we are all in bother. Such actions open up the system to abuses and this can't be good for the game.

The Crown Office in Edinburgh did warn football that if there wasn't greater control they would step in. But I repeat that although I appreciate that none of us is above the law, I believe Scottish football can only be run in an orderly way without outside help or interference. In fact, behaviour at Scottish grounds has improved dramatically. The Criminal Justice (Scotland) Bill, which prevents supporters taking drink into grounds, or indeed watching if they have over-indulged, has been a superb help in the campaign to restore a family atmosphere at matches. At Parkhead we have regular meetings with the police, stewards and the supporters' associations, and the success which has been achieved in bringing people back to the grounds across Scotland must indicate football authorities are on the right track. We're not perfect, but hopefully one day we will come close. The vast improvement in atmosphere and conduct at grounds is something we must continue to work on.

What happened at Ibrox — the ordered intervention of the police — created a lot of resentment. Football was obviously picked out for this special treatment because it is the biggest spectator sport. But where does it end? Does a jockey hitting an opponent with his whip during a race appear in court for assault? What about ice-hockey players who charge into each other without mercy? Will a policeman step into a boxing ring and say one of the contestants was guilty of a low blow and will, therefore, be required to appear at the police station? The mechanics for

Celtic's 1987-88 pool at the start of the season.
Standing: Smith, Morris, O'Leary, McKnight, Stark, McGugan, McCarthy,
Bonner, Whyte, Rogan, Burns.
Sitting: McStay, Grant, Shepherd, Aitken, McGhee, Walker, Archdeacon.

discipline exist in sport and they have got to be supported.

It seems appropriate to say here that I do not agree with the SFA system of automatic punishments. My personal opinion is that we should incline much more towards reasonable fines for the players and, if necessary, clubs and managers. Under the present disciplinary system I wonder at times who is being punished. When players miss games the club suffers and so do the spectators. It is surely significant that the Scottish PFA have given clubs a list of suggested fines for players involved in trouble with referees. For instance, a first offender for dissent — talking back to the referee and other misdemeanours like kicking the ball away — should lose ten per cent of his wages. Sending-off starts at 25 per cent and goes right up to a total loss of pay for persistent offenders. Remember, these are the representatives of the players who are saying this. They clearly see fines as the best deterrent.

If, in the judgment of the SFA, a club fail to keep their team under control then the manager and perhaps the chairman should be summoned. The SFA could spell out faults and the code of practice required. If this was further breached the club and, if necessary, the manager, would be fined. The present system penalises the club and spectators much more than the players. I also feel when dealing with pitch incidents the offence must be examined neutrally and fairly in the cold light of day. I have no patience with players who are booked for stupidities like petulantly kicking or throwing the ball away. But I do recognise that players will be booked during games because they have entered into the spirit of the contest.

In fact, I don't like fining players and last season I had to do it on very few occasions. However, money out of their pay packets is the most salutary method of teaching them a lesson. Clearly, I can't pontificate about behaviour without accepting that, as a manager, I must lead by example or, if I slip up, face the same kind of discipline. Immediate responsibility for discipline must lie with the manager. So if a team has a bad record he can't just walk away from his responsibilities.

There is at present no appeal against a referee's decision. This is wrong. There should be an avenue to challenge a faultily administered red or yellow card with a monetary penalty if an appeal is found to be frivolous.

Without being even remotely smug it is reasonable to point out that Celtic had 31 yellow cards and three orderings-off last season. This was the smallest number of cautions in the Premier League of 12 clubs. Morton, for instance, had 66 yellow cards, St Mirren 60, Hearts 54 and Rangers and Aberdeen 45 apiece. Rangers also had four sent off.

Going back to the controversial Ibrox meeting, we lost a last-minute goal which levelled the score at 2-2 with our ten men playing against nine. It was the ideal occasion to win with some panache, despite the earlier incidents, but we simply didn't finish the job off. Billy Stark had a great header which came off the underside of the bar, but quoting this should not be interpreted as excuse-making. We should never have lost a point and all of us knew it.

We couldn't yet shake off this disappointing period. Back home we slipped up 2-1 to Dundee United and then we were 3-0 up against Falkirk and lost two late goals. We had to fight to hold on at 3-2. All sorts of questions were being asked about the team and the fans were making their demands. This was when I had to exercise the determination to do what I thought was right. There had been loud and persistent chanting from the crowd during the game at Falkirk demanding that I sign Charlie Nicholas. I realised that this was the classic time for a weak manager to surrender. But, in my view, it was also the testing ground for the season in many ways. What chance had the players of succeeding if the boss didn't keep his cool? We had gone through a rocky, six-match spell in which very little went right from the time we were knocked out of Europe. We dropped five points by drawing three times and losing once.

So it was with some apprehension that we went to Aberdeen at the end of October with me standing firmly by my beliefs. Frank McAvennie scored in a 1-0 win and Mick McCarthy also had a spectacular 90 minutes. He had struggled up to then after suffering a bad injury. He needed to set the place on fire — and did. From there we went to Tynecastle where McCarthy fell from grace by being sent off, but we fought back with our gallant ten for a 1-1 draw, with Mark McGhee getting the leveller.

Then we got the break we needed. At just the right time Aberdeen relented and sold Joe Miller to us. On 14 November we played Dundee and Miller's first touch told me that he was the player to put the finishing edge to our side. And, in addition to this, he confirmed that Parkhead was the place for him to play. In the first couple of minutes a ball was knocked out to him near the touchline and he pulled it down gracefully and passed it beautifully across the face of the goal. Celtic won 5-0 with Andy Walker and Frank McAvennie getting two each and Miller himself completing the total.

Motherwell tumbled 2-0, Dunfermline 4-0, and we worked hard to beat both St Mirren and Hibs 1-0. Style and confidence was in Celtic's play. Morton fell 4-0 and McAvennie scored all four, which must have convinced doubters that he was the right man for the job. Then we came back from the dead to draw 2-2 with Hearts, thanks to an Andy Walker penalty and a Paul McStay equaliser. One disappointment was a goalless draw with Aberdeen because it was a poor game watched by nearly 32,000. However, one thing had been established and that was that nobody would beat us easily. We weren't a soft touch any more. From then on in things began to fall into place.

We won four more points by beating Falkirk 2-0 and Dundee United 2-1. Both games were away from home which made the performances even more satisfactory. It was a good run-up to the most vital game of the season — at Parkhead on 2 January 1988. This was a meeting which meant a great deal to both sets of fans because Graeme Souness still harboured thoughts that Rangers could come off the floor and keep the championship at Ibrox.

We trained on New Year's morning, which was a Friday, spent a bit of time at the Park and then drove to the Crest Hotel at Erskine. I felt our preparation was just right. We didn't concern ourselves with any of the other matches. Nor did we even watch the TV sports programmes. I was sure on Saturday morning that we would win. I could see the evidence all around me. The faces of the players and their attitude to the upcoming game told me.

Rangers pulled a stroke by signing Mark Walters and playing him against us. Walters was well known to me because I had him on my staff at Aston Villa although he had an unlucky spell of injuries at that time. In fact, I was very nearly present at his signing for Rangers. Jack McGinn and I lunched at the Excelsior Hotel, at Glasgow Airport, with David Holmes and Graeme Souness to talk about new pre-match arrangements to try to ensure peace among the crowd. The players were to walk out together, mingle at the kick-about and generally demonstrate that the teams were contestants in a football match and not bitter personal enemies. We had a pleasant lunch — there is no reason why it shouldn't have been so. I feel there should always be good relations between the two clubs. However, I did feel at the time that there was another factor in the wind. I said to my chairman as we left: "There's something happening . . . Rangers are going to sign somebody." Not long afterwards I found out Graeme had waited on to meet Walters coming off the Birmingham plane and had taken him to Ibrox for the signing. I didn't let this bother or distract me.

At any rate, we won the game 2-0 and I felt it was one of the more convincing wins that Celtic have had over Rangers, with Frank McAvennie scoring both goals. I believed from then onwards that winning the League was in our own hands. I never at any time said to the players during the season that we would be champions — even when this was being shouted by others from the rooftops. But, privately, I was sure it was in the bag if we kept our cool. I adopted the style of discussing only our next game and never projecting any farther than this. All we had to do was keep winning and nobody could touch us. The victory over Rangers, and the style of it, was the biggest morale boost we could have had.

The following week we managed only a draw with St Mirren and that was thanks to an own goal by Campbell Money, the Saints 'keeper. He palmed a cross by Chris Morris into his own net. From then on in we were in control. Of course we stumbled, but that's part of the hazard of winning the League. It's a myth to imagine a club can triumph only by playing brilliantly every week. It doesn't happen in reality. What Celtic did was to show an outstanding determination not to lose too many matches. From the Rangers game at the turn of the year we conceded only five League goals. The single-mindedness of the players was brilliant. At this point I realised the full extent of the progress Celtic had made since the start of the season. Young players had matured and we were a hardened crew.

We went six points clear of Rangers with eight matches to play in a live televised Sunday game in March. Paul McStay scored for Celtic and then Jan Bartram, the controversial Dane, equalised. Our winner came with 11 minutes to go when the ball was deflected off Andy Walker's chest and swirled out of Chris Woods' reach.

The only time our concentration really broke in the run-in was after our dramatic win over Hearts in the Scottish Cup semi-final. We went to Tynecastle in the League the following week and it was possibly inevitable that something would go wrong. Mike Galloway and Gary Mackay scored and our only reply was from Mark McGhee. However, we won the game which mattered more — the Cup-tie. It didn't displease me badly to drop two points because we had gone so long without losing. We knew that we had three games in which to get one point to clinch the title. As it happened, we didn't need that extra point because Hearts drew their next game and we were champions anyway.

The game — or was it a gigantic party? — every Celtic fan in the world wanted to see was our meeting on 23 April 1988 with Dundee at Parkhead. A 3-0 defeat of Dundee gave our fans something to remember for a long, long time. The crowd was given officially as 60,800 — a fantastic attendance by any standard — but

What more could I ask? The Championship Trophy in one hand and about to congratulate captain Roy Aitken with the other. Chairman Jack McGinn turns to speak to retiring League president Ian Gallatly, who handed over the silverware.

there seemed to be supporters everywhere and it was a smashing birthday party afternoon. The crowd chanted "Happy birthday . . . happy birthday" and refused to leave until I came out with the players 15 minutes after the game had ended. I was still wearing a track suit and hadn't been in the bath, but nobody cared about such details. This was the first time the fans were seeing the team on home territory as the 1988 champions. It was a record 35th championship for Celtic and was my fourth as a manager plus nine previously while playing.

I realised my message to the players about the standards needed at Celtic Park had been driven home in the very last League game against Dunfermline. Chris Morris scored a stunning goal early on and the game died. There was never any danger of Dunfermline scoring, but when the players came to the dressing-room they were flat and disappointed. They hadn't turned on that final bit of style for the customers. I had to say to them: "Hey, you've won the League. Would you have settled for this at the start?" However, that's when I knew they had set the highest standards themselves

31

and that they were annoyed personally when these dropped. We had been on such a high against Dundee. Then we beat Motherwell and had only the Fifers to meet before the Scottish Cup final a week later. The fact that Celtic won those last three League games with the final looming spoke volumes for the professionalism of the players.

The championship trophy was handed over at the Dunfermline match by the retiring League president Ian Gellatly. I was delighted. We had already achieved the top place in the League before this match but deliberately held off the presentation until the last match. The realisation of being champions and the ceremony were smashing. The package was great. I think it is worth reproducing the League table. Forgive me if I again draw attention to our record total of 72 points.

	P	W	D	L	F	A	W	D	L	F	A	Pts
Celtic	44	16	5	1	42	11	15	5	2	37	12	72
Hearts	44	13	8	1	37	17	10	8	4	37	15	62
Rangers	44	14	4	4	49	17	12	4	6	36	17	60
Aberdeen	44	11	7	4	27	11	10	10	2	29	14	59
Dundee Utd	44	8	7	7	29	24	8	8	6	25	23	47
Hibernian	44	8	8	6	18	17	4	11	7	23	25	43
Dundee	44	9	5	8	31	25	8	2	12	39	39	41
Motherwell	44	10	2	10	25	31	3	8	11	12	25	36
St Mirren	44	5	11	6	22	28	5	4	13	19	36	35
Falkirk	44	8	4	10	26	35	2	7	13	15	40	31
Dunfermline	44	6	6	10	23	35	2	4	16	18	49	26
Morton	44	3	7	12	19	47	0	3	19	8	53	16

I have been asked how the current side compares with the Lisbon Lions. The question is really unfair because it will never be answered by the sides meeting. However, what I will say about my Centenary Doublers is that they are as determined as the Lions and they also have the same kind of feeling for each other. This was demonstrated in full by the fact that Pat Bonner's injury in the week of the Cup final was kept so secret that I didn't even tell my wife about it! The players realised the importance of Pat's situation to the team and they did what I asked and said absolutely nothing until the news was given out before the match that Allen McKnight would be in our goal. The pundits didn't have a whisper about it.

For the first time we involved ourselves in a wee bit of commercialism. We allowed TV cameras on the team coach from Seamill to Hampden. This kind of thing worried me. Finally, I said

I would allow it provided the players assured me they wouldn't let the cameras interfere in any way with their preparation, application and dedication for the big game. They reassured me, saying nothing would deflect from the final — and it didn't. This proved they had grown up as a team. Their approach was adult.

It wasn't easy in the Cup. Our third-round draw against lowly Stranraer was about the worst we could have had, because they hadn't won for ages and a wee team coming to Parkhead with this kind of record is worrying. I would rather have played them at Stranraer. Anyway, we were fortunate not to have had to replay instead of winning with a Frank McAvennie goal. I had discussed the Cup with the players and told them to set their sights on getting to the Hampden final. We could talk about winning later. In the next round we had a goalless draw at home to Hibs but I knew, I really did, that we would win the replay at Easter Road and, thankfully, Billy Stark proved me right with a goal. Andy Walker, Tommy Burns and Stark again scored in the quarter-final with Partick Thistle which saw Firhill full to capacity with a crowd of 16,800.

When I looked at the semi-final draw — Aberdeen versus Dundee United and Celtic against Hearts — I said that whatever happened it was going to be a good final. Celtic hadn't lost a goal in four ties. We brought forward a game against St Mirren to Cup semi week. It was a risk, but worth taking because it allowed Frank McAvennie to work off a one-game disciplinary ban. So he was able to play against Hearts.

In the first half of that match we thought we were the better side. But I said at half-time that we weren't playing as well as we could. It was up to us to put this right. "If we want to get to the final let's go out and do it," I said in the dressing-room. However, in the second half Celtic lost a goal in a controversial situation. Then we took over. Mark McGhee came on for Joe Miller. Before and after his appearance Celtic missed chances. With a couple of minutes to go the easiest thing to do when McGhee equalised would have been to hold on for a replay. But my players didn't want to know about a draw. McGhee headed the ball down and Andy Walker scored. People said it was luck. Of course there was an element of this. But there was also the appetite of Celtic for winning. The determination of the team is as good as or better than any I have come against before.

Alex MacDonald, the Hearts manager, said to the Press later that his team had "blown it". Having lost the League two years before to Celtic in the last game when Hearts were beaten at Dundee as Celtic walloped St Mirren, I could understand how Alex felt. However, we won a lot of matches in the last few minutes and I was happy to prove the critics who said we were a first-half team wrong.

And so to Hampden for the 103rd final. I'm sure the spectators who watched in a 70,000 crowd will remember the game for a long time to come. Had it been scripted for TV I doubt if the most imaginative writer could have produced a better finale.

One unfortunate outcome from the brought-forward St Mirren game was an injury to Peter Grant. The immediate reaction was that he had no chance of playing against Dundee United in the final after missing the semi. But I knew deep down that Peter would do everything in his power to be ready. He broke a bone in his foot but he got the plaster off earlier than anybody anticipated. I played him in a reserve game against Dunfermline on a Friday night and then brought him on for the last 25 minutes in the Premier League match with the Fifers next day.

Then we were left with a week in which there were no games and I wanted to give Peter every chance for the final. So I arranged a closed-doors game with Queen's Park at Parkhead. The object was to find out about his fitness. I wanted him to show me he was fit. At the end of the match there was no doubt in my mind that Peter was short of his best but I also had to decide if lack of crowd atmosphere had anything to do with it.

On the Tuesday night I knew Peter wouldn't play at Hampden. I had to be fair to the others and couldn't take a risk with a player, even one so good, whose fitness was a gamble. I still watched his every move at Seamill. I studied him walking, training, going into small-sided games, and all in the hope that he would show me I was wrong. But on the Friday I had to tell him he wasn't playing. I could see he was all welled-up inside. It was an awful decision to have to take but it was the only one that was right for Celtic.

We already had the worry of Pat Bonner, who had a calf-muscle injury. On Friday I told Allen McKnight he had to prepare as though he was playing the next day. I told Allen I would let him know in the morning. Possibly it was unfair to leave him wondering all night but there was no other way. Pat's injury was camouflaged from everybody as physio Brian Scott tried to get him fit. Nobody except those who had to know was aware of what was happening. I worked Pat quite hard in the morning and then asked how he felt. He told me he wasn't 100 per cent and I replied that he had taken the hard decision. So Allen played and he certainly didn't let us down.

It was typical of the attitude of the team. They all worked so hard together they didn't want to risk letting each other down. Before the game I told the whole team I had the feeling the final would be a 13-man operation. And that's the way it turned out.

Kevin Gallacher scored a very good goal for Dundee United three minutes into the second half. It was a superb shot. Roy Aitken was running beside him but, having had his name taken shortly before, the risk of a tackle and a foul which could have led to him being sent off was too great. Roy tried to jockey him on the run instead but Gallacher was going fast and was in no mood to lose the ball. So we were back in the position of being a goal down. I decided to make my substitutions in the 69th minute. Billy Stark and Mark McGhee went on to replace Derek Whyte and Andy Walker.

The final 15 minutes were something of a personal triumph for Frank McAvennie. In the 75th minute he headed the equaliser from Anton Rogan's cross. And what a game the full-back had, by the way. It was his best for Celtic. United hung on courageously but Celtic didn't fancy the idea of extra time or a replay and Frank struck a great winning shot with only seconds to go as referee George Smith glanced at his watch.

We had slightly the better of the first half, when Joe Miller missed a great chance with a header. In many ways it was a tense and nervous game. It needed something to bring it alive and — bingo! — Gallacher got his goal which caught us on the hop coming out. It was magnificent play in a Cup final. That was when the big decisions had to be made. I was prepared to leave Celtic short at the back. I said to Tommy Craig: "Right now we've lost the Cup . . . we've got to go out and win it." That's why I brought Stark on to give Joe freedom on the other side. Andy Walker had probably been asked for too much during the season so I changed him for

Roy obviously believed we had our names on the Scottish Cup just handed to him by Mrs Thatcher.

Mark McGhee's strength and determination. We stretched United and stretched ourselves. Stark was creating width on the right, wee Joe started to run at Dave Bowman and Mark's strength began to tell. The back four also told themselves they had lost one goal and wouldn't concede another. As soon as we levelled I knew we would win — maybe in extra time but we looked stronger and fitter.

It pleased me that the first on the pitch at the finish were Peter Grant, Lex Baillie, Pat Bonner, and substituted players Andy

36

Walker and Derek Whyte. I had said I wanted all of them in the dug-out during the game because everyone had played a part in the success. Even if we had lost there was plenty to celebrate. Celtic had won the League so I knew we could smile no matter what happened against United. But it indicated the depth of team spirit that the lads in the dug-out were first to congratulate the guys who had just played.

At that point I went to the dressing-room. I was alone there with my thoughts. But I also wanted the players to be out on the pitch and have their moments of triumph because they had won the Cup, not me. It is unlike me to want to be by myself but for once I did. Eventually Jack McGinn came in and said: "I think they want you out there, Billy."

Back in the dressing-room afterwards the players were quite subdued. The only mistake we had made in our preparation was forgetting to bring champagne. So we had to borrow some bottles from Queen's Park. Then we all went back to Parkhead and had a smashing get-together and finally my pals Mike Jackson, Benny Rooney and Gordon Whitelaw came to my home to round the night off.

I felt a little sorry for United. It was their fifth defeat in five finals. But a match like this is a selfish occasion. There can be only one winner. I wanted it to be Celtic. I couldn't believe it in the end. In 12 months I had gone from one extreme as a manager to the other — booted by Aston Villa and now lauded by Celtic after the first double victory in my management career. That Centenary Double will go down in the rolls of Celtic history and the players will be remembered in the same way as the European Cup winners of 1967. That is great for them and I feel very proud.

Each of the players used in our campaign was outstanding. For this reason I am reluctant to individualise, but none would argue about the fact that Paul McStay was superb. When I took over at Celtic again I worried about him leaving the club. There were a lot of pressures on him from many sources to go. Where we were fortunate was that his dad, John, was involved in all the discussions we had with Paul and he advised him wisely.

Paul got a good deal for staying with Celtic but he is entitled to it. He is a great asset and I feel there's more to come, much more, from this talented young man. He is the one player in Scotland who

Rhapsody in Green as Tommy Craig holds the Scottish Cup aloft. My laugh was was fairly hearty that day.

currently has the opportunity to be world-class. He has still to prove this but he will have benefited from our success.

John gave me a boost when the signing took place in December. He said that had I not gone back to Parkhead his boy might well have moved. He added that he could see success ahead and, for that reason, Paul was all the more delighted to stay. In his opinion Paul had played his best football since my return. Well, I like to think that when I'm an old man there will be a lot of players whom I've introduced into first-class football who reach a situation where they are very comfortably off because of their ability on the pitch.

I feel almost embarrassed when I talk about Roy Aitken. Paul has captured much of the limelight but I doubt if Roy has had a better season. He is expected to play well as a matter of course and he rarely lets anybody down. He has been magnificent.

Of the others, Frank McAvennie has scored outstanding goals, Peter Grant is a youngster who is developing, Derek Whyte is still not 20 and is fast improving, and Anton Rogan learns with every game. Pat Bonner is a smashing 'keeper and it's maybe not surprising that Celtic's goals against total was the lowest achieved by the club since 1925. Chris Morris, Billy Stark, Tommy Burns, Andy Walker . . . oh, I could go on and on but collectively the team have worked brilliantly. Their spirit is outstandingly high.

I think we'll reap an even greater benefit from our players. Celtic have never been more ambitious as a club. This is evident at every level. The lads are delighted with the Double but they have been reminded that winning is a habit. We must keep it as an important part of our nature and personality. Celtic will continue to be a good side because we have a lot of players who have learned excellent lessons from the 1988 double event.

As a matter of record here are the players used by Celtic in the League campaign — Pat Bonner, Chris Morris, Anton Rogan, Roy Aitken, Mick McCarthy, Derek Whyte, Peter Grant, Billy Stark, Paul McStay, Tommy Burns, Frank McAvennie, Andy Walker, Joe Miller, Owen Archdeacon, Mark McGhee, Allen McKnight, Dugald McCarrison, Lex Baillie, Paul McGugan, Dougie McGuire and Tony Shepherd. And in that great and unforgettable Scottish Cup final the line-ups were — *Celtic*: McKnight, Morris, Aitken, McCarthy, Whyte, Stark (s69), Rogan, McStay, Burns, Miller, McAvennie, Walker, McGhee (s69). *Dundee United*: Thomson, Bowman, Hegarty, Narey, Malpas, McKinlay, McInally, Bannon, Ferguson, Paatelainen, Clark (s70), Gallacher. Sub: Sturrock (not used).

Chapter Two

In the Beginning

I DIDN'T know about the delights and disappointments ahead of me the first time I went to see Celtic as an eight-year-old. But I should have had an inkling as my Auntie Grace, who took me to Paradise, lost her shoe in the "jungle".

In that first visit to Parkhead Celtic beat Aberdeen 4-2 and Charlie Tully scored twice. One of the goals was a header and he didn't do that too often. I wrote to my Dad, who was then in the Army in West Africa, about the game. In my excitement I got the first names of Tully the wrong way round and called him Patrick Charles.

Tully was the nearest thing to a superstar I had seen. The Irishman was extra special — a genius on the pitch and star turn for the gentlemen of the Press off it. There was a hysteria about him. It is my first memory of fan idolatry. He was the Charlie Nicholas or Jimmy Johnstone of his time — and then some. Years later I was told that when Tully went to see the première of the film *Bonnie Prince Charlie* he walked out when he discovered it wasn't about him.

We stood in the "jungle" that day when it was still the old cowshed. There were no crush barriers so the crowd moved involuntarily up and down the terracing. My Auntie Grace didn't know what to do when she lost her shoe but there was certainly no way she could find it among all those fans. There was nothing else for it. She had to go home on the public service bus with only one shoe.

Shortly after that I was taken to see Celtic against Albion Rovers. It was a 3-3 draw. But the significance was that the Rovers'

40

centre-half was Jock Stein. I didn't pick him out at the time but years later the game cropped up in conversation in our dressing-room and Big Jock recalled every detail.

My dad, Jimmy, a straight-backed, very fit 22-year army man who began with the Black Watch and finished in the Army Physical Training Corps as a WO II, was strict with me. I was an only son but wasn't spoiled. That big rough place called Glasgow was out of bounds unless somebody took me the ten or 12 miles from Bellshill.

My dad wouldn't allow me to wear a Celtic scarf. Not that he minded me supporting Celtic — there was simply something too emotive for him about flaunting loyalties in this way. I mostly had to watch Motherwell, in fact, because it was the most convenient ground. The covered enclosure which is now opposite the main stand at Fir Park didn't exist in those days and the only vantage point for little lads was up trees on the perimeter of the ground.

I was 13 or 14 before I was allowed to go to Glasgow with my pals to see Celtic. We took the train from Bellshill and walked when we got to the city. My dad once caught me, about to set off for a match, wearing Celtic colours. I had bought the scarf with my pocket-money. When I saw him I got a real fright. He made me go home and take it off — or else!

I certainly have no regrets whatever about my upbringing. My parents did everything they could for me. Because of Dad my basic principles in life have never wavered. I'm glad now. Although ours was a Catholic household I was never allowed to think that Catholics were supreme. Bellshill was a mining community and the people inter-mixed well. It was a community in every sense. If I had tried to make a distinction between Catholics and non-Catholics I would have had my backside well and truly booted. My father kept hammering on about principles and I benefited from it. My mother, Ellen, doted on me as, I suppose, mothers tend to do with only children. She never enjoyed watching me playing football. I think she was always too worried that I would get hurt. She has always been proud of me and I have the same feelings for her.

I also inherited my politics from my parents. I have always been a Socialist and don't see that whatever success I have had should change this. I continue to vote Labour. Remembering one's background is important and mine is very definitely working-class.

I don't think, either, that I'm viewing the Labour Party from afar. Mrs Thatcher, whom I met at the Scottish Cup final when she was the guest of honour, represents everything that I disagree with in politics. Because of her lack of success in Scotland I honestly believe she does everything in her power to upset us. She is obviously a very clever woman but she is totally opposed to anything I've ever believed in or stood for.

Apart from a short spell in an Army barracks at Hereford, where the SAS are now based, I spent most of my childhood in Bellshill. Dad didn't want to interfere with my schooling but in Hereford I went to a rugby-playing school and really enjoyed it.

When we returned to Bellshill — my dad had been posted to Cowglen Hospital to look after the rehabilitation of soldiers — we lived with my grandparents and Auntie Grace, whose real name was Ursula, though everyone knew her as Grace. My grandparents on my mother Ellen's side were in fact Lithuanian and once when I played in Kiev, in the Ukraine, Soviet journalists came to interview me about this. Anyway we all lived in a miners' row. My mum, dad and I shared the back room. The others occupied the big room off the kitchen which had two bed recesses. There was an outside toilet — and I really mean outside. Later we moved to a prefab.

The house I live in now on the south side of Glasgow is rather different. But thinking back only makes me appreciate luxuries that bit more. So, with this background, and parents who were strict but gave me a smashing upbringing, there is no chance of me ever losing my sense of proportion.

I've been back to Hereford only once since I spent 2½ years at the High School and before that St Francis Xavier Primary, but my memories of the English town are vivid. It was the only time in my dad's soldiering career that I was in married quarters with my mum. A couple of SAS men used to come to Maine Road when I was manager of Manchester City and they invited me to visit their barracks — the same place I had lived in years before. Unfortunately, I didn't get the chance to see the town or visit my old schools.

Our Lady's at Motherwell had the most impact on my education and early footballing. Newspapers had begun to take an interest in schools football at the time I was beginning to make headway. Our

Playing for the jersey — and watching the ball.

Lady's was very football-minded and there was a lot of excitement when we played Holyrood in the Scottish Schools Cup final. It ended in a draw at Hampden. For some reason the replay was scheduled for Blantyre Victoria's ground which the headmasters said was unsuitable. So the final was never completed, greatly to my disappointment. The irony was that later, when I signed for Celtic, I was 'farmed out' to Blantyre Vics. This was also Jock Stein's junior club. Our paths began to cross and kept on doing so.

I had trials with Arsenal and Manchester United and there were various approaches from Scots clubs. When I was with Vics Rangers inquired about me but I won't tell you how I was described to them. It had something to do with my religion. They didn't pursue their interest. My parish priest, Father Butler, thought I should go to Clyde. He supported them, by the way. I probably wouldn't have signed for them even if Celtic hadn't come along, but I was saved the trouble of making a decision. Clyde didn't think I was good enough. I used to 'dig up' the late Willie Dunn, the chairman at Shawfield, about the assessment. He had a good laugh. Later, of course, I began my career as a manager with Clyde for a short spell.

I recall Davie Meiklejohn, a former great Ranger and manager of Partick Thistle, offering me a tenner a week on a gentlemen's agreement to go to Firhill. That was a lot of money at the time, but my dad wouldn't have anything to do with unwritten cash deals.

My future was settled when I played at Parkhead for Scotland's secondary schools against England whom we beat 3-0. Jock Stein was at the game. Along with one of the club's scouts, Eddie McCardle, he persuaded Sir Robert Kelly, the Celtic chairman and very much the dominant figure at the club, to sign me. Eddie was also a teacher at St Joseph's and was the Provost of Motherwell.

Celtic, it emerged, had decided on two other centre-halves ahead of me — George Gunn, of Holyrood, and John Curran, of St Mungo's. However, I was chosen as the centre-half to meet the England schools team ahead of them although George was the right-back. Big Jock's influence in my signing meant a personal involvement in my future.

It was Big Jock and Mr McCardle who came to my home to discuss me becoming a provisional Celtic signing. There wasn't any haggling! There were some interesting names in that Scottish side.

Craig Brown, now the assistant to Andy Roxburgh, Billy Little (Aberdeen), Hugh Brown (Kilmarnock), Ian Lochhead (Celtic), Dave Hilley (Third Lanark) and Brian McIlroy (Rangers) were all there. Interestingly Billy Little and I went to Newcastle at one point to look at prospects. He said he wouldn't sign for an English club because it was too far away from his home in Dumfries. It always struck me as funny that he ended up going to Aberdeen.

I have happy memories about spending a good part of 1957 with Vics. The late Joe Gans, father of Walter McGowan, the ex-world champion boxer, helped with the training. He was quite a character. I was 17 and had stayed on at Our Lady's to get highers in English, Maths and Spanish. I enjoyed school as Our Lady's was good for football as well as academically. Looking back on what I've done with my life, the one bit I would change, in fact, is missing university. I'm sorry about this. It is an important gap. My big regret is that it's probably too late to rectify the situation.

1958 was the World Cup finals in Sweden. Traditonally in those days, Celtic went to Ireland at the end of a season to play on both sides of the Border. Bobby Evans, Willie Fernie and Bobby Collins were in the Scotland squad so I was pulled in to go on the Irish trip. My first Celtic reserve game had been against Rangers and Don (The Rhino) Kichenbrand, sensation of the late Fifties, was the opposing centre-forward. Imagine my surprise when he also lined up against me for a Bohemians Select in Dublin. Kichenbrand was hugely successful in a fairly brief spell at Ibrox. He now works for Richard Gough's father in homeland South Africa and, in fact, it was he who recommended Richard to clubs in Scotland. Meanwhile we next went to Belfast and played against a Select side in a testimonial for a player called Johnny Campbell, and from there to Derry City. All this was great experience for me.

I returned to Parkhead ready to continue my apprenticeship. But after three reserve games Bobby Evans was injured at the same time as centre-half John Jack, so I was drafted into the top side. We beat Clyde 2-0 at Parkhead. I then stayed in for a few more matches at centre-half but I was being brought along carefully.

That season we got to the semi-final of the League Cup but lost at Ibrox to Partick Thistle. After that I was in and out of the team. I played right-half, right-back and centre-half, which was a smashing grounding for an 18-year-old. Around this time Jock Stein retired from playing. An ankle injury left him with a slight, but permanent, limp. He had always taken a terrific interest in youngsters like myself.

We had a squad of daft laddies. I signed on the same day as Pat Crerand and Andy Murphy. We quickly joined in with such as Mike Jackson, John Divers, John Colrain, Bertie Auld and Matt McVittie. We were all about the same age and hung on every word Big Jock said. Celtic's team lunched every day in a restaurant at the top of Buchanan Street. It was also a talk shop. We were able to listen to Neilly Mochan, Bertie Peacock, Willie Fernie, Bobby Collins and Big Jock giving their opinions about football. We didn't say a word, only listened. They were very senior men and it would not have been right for us to throw in our views.

These were the days when clubs held public trials before each season started. At Parkhead, I had to oppose Billy McPhail which was a big job for a lad. I did well, though, and Bobby Collins took a tremendous interest in me. He wasn't at Parkhead much longer, but in the short period before he moved to England he was very helpful to me. What a trainer he was!

At the time there were some really big names at Parkhead. Think of some: Charlie Tully, John Higgins, Sean Fallon, Sammy Wilson, Bobby Evans and Johnny Bonnar. Listening to them blethering about football was an education.

Reflecting on the way I was thrown into the League team at intervals I wonder if we prepare kids too much nowadays. They must appreciate, however talented they may be leaving school, that they are very much at the bottom of an apprenticeship ladder. One of the reasons they find it difficult on entering professional sport is that they have been so protected and made to feel important in their age-group.

Until I won my first cap in the infamous 9-3 drubbing from England at Wembley, I was part-time. I worked for Lanarkshire County Council at Hamilton in the revaluation department and then moved to a job with Stenhouse, the insurance company, in Glasgow. I thought nothing of leaving home at 7.30 a.m. to work and then going to Parkhead at six in the evening to train. Early arrivals got a good pair of stockings and training shoes. The others had to make do with what was left. We had fisherman-type jerseys and black pants with no understrip. Celtic reserves could be identified by the red weals on their necks from the rubbing of the coarse jerseys.

Training consisted of running round the park and in winter there was only one light on the corner of the stand. No floodlights in these days. It was all running and sprinting. On really wet nights we were allowed into the gym and played with ten or 12 a side. Training consisted of the bare essentials.

I think boys are spoiled now because senior clubs are so desperate to get the best out of them. We are competing to sign them when they are at a very early age so we have to offer the best facilities and equipment. I don't think it is necessarily right but under the present system there isn't any alternative. There is a danger of over-preparing kids. We are also making them too secure and too comfortable too early. It would be better if there were fewer competitive games for wee boys. Let them learn without being under the pressure of having to win.

A problem can be that parents, with the best intentions, want to see their sons winning medals. This is understandable. But is it wise? It might be better if they held back and let them enjoy learning the game. My son, Martyn, is enthusiastic, but I'll let him develop in the game if he wants to without pressure from me.

When I was small — I was once! — we played in the streets. There weren't too many cars in a miners' row so we had plenty of room. In the cities the boys practised in the back courts. That's why Scotland produced players like Willie Fernie, Jimmy Johnstone and Willie Henderson who were classic dribblers with the ball.

I remember in the early Fifties it was almost embarrassing to be a Celtic fan as the club were having such a bad run. Then along came the Coronation Cup and Celtic beat Hibs 2-0 in the final. Neilly Mochan scored a wonderful goal. He had one of the most powerful left-foot shots in the game. His super goal was from 25 yards but when we talk about it now it has stretched to 55 yards. The date was 20 May 1953, and the game was seen by 107,000 as part of the celebrations for the coronation of our present Queen. Neilly was certainly 'King' in my eyes for the way he beat the Hibs 'keeper Tommy Younger. Jock Stein was the Celtic skipper and, after a second goal by Jimmy Walsh, he took the trophy to cheering Hampden can no longer match. The victory fairly boosted the morale of youngsters like me. The teams which so entranced us were: *Celtic*: Bonnar, Haughney, Rollo, Evans, Stein, McPhail, Collins, Walsh, Mochan, Peacock, Fernie. *Hibs*: Younger, Govan, Paterson, Buchanan, Howie, Combe, Smith, Johnstone, Reilly, Turnbull, Ormond.

Ironically, I got into the Celtic team regularly only when I started to put real pressure on Bobby Evans who played in that match. Despite the fact the he was centre-half for Scotland this wasn't his position. He was a right-half who would be called a right-side midfielder today. He was a hero of mine, ever so industrious and totally committed.

I played in the same side as Bobby from time to time and it gave me first-hand knowledge of his ability and worth. I often wondered why Celtic let him go to Chelsea. But Big Jock once told me that Evans did things he wouldn't accept from a genuine centre-half. That was when we youngsters sat beside him during games and he made points to us about the play. Bobby tended to back off centre-forwards — strikers to you — and Big Jock's belief, and mine, is that the centre-half must attack the ball and the earlier the better. When we talk about skills this is usually related to clever forwards who pull the ball down, beat a man and shoot. But good defending is a skill, too, and equally important. It was odd hearing Big Jock telling me not to copy the style of such a famous player.

I finally received a Scottish cap on 15 April 1961. We met England at Wembley in that 9-3 nightmare in which Johnny Haynes ripped us apart. In those days international teams weren't selected on continuity but because somebody decided who was in form with their clubs. There was some high-class talent at Wembley. The lineups were: *England*: Springett, Armfield, McNeil, Robson, Swan, Flowers, Douglas, Greaves, Smith, Haynes, Charlton. *Scotland*: Haffey, Shearer, Caldow, Mackay, McNeill, McCann, McLeod, Law, St. John, Quinn, Wilson.

Playing was such a big honour for me it was an incredible feeling. I was still a part-timer, although I decided immediately afterwards to concentrate all my efforts on football. Dave Mackay, who to this day remains one of the best players I've known both from a personality and practical point of view, said as we went on to Wembley: "If we can't play here, we can't play anywhere." Dave was in the Spurs side which won the double that year. Like Celtic, they were playing in the Cup final a week after the international.

Wembley was a disaster for Scotland. A tartan blot on the history of England-Scotland games. Haynes was truly outstanding but there were other smashing players like Jimmy Greaves, who scored a hat-trick. Jimmy certainly had no inkling then that years later he would team up with Ian St. John for a TV double act.

Scotland fought back to 3-2 with a goal by Davy Wilson early in the second half. But England then got a free-kick near the penalty area which we disputed. Bryan Douglas, in my opinion, moved the ball five yards from where the infringement took place. The referee let him take the kick all the same and he scored. So we went 4-2 down and any hope of turning the game around went up in smoke. In fact, we lost the place as a team. The English cavalry charged right through us. I felt like the country boy come to town for the first time.

It was a Saturday game and afterwards, under cover of darkness, we went out to some wee club in London where they charged extortionately for jugs of beer. Ian St. John, Bert McCann, Pat Quinn, Dunky MacKay and myself tried to drown our sorrows. We had visas to go to Czechoslovakia later in the World Cup. Bert McCann suggested burning them as we wouldn't be going. Bert put a match to his but the rest of us chickened out. The headlines in the Sunday papers next day spelt it out: "World Cup pool is scrapped." However, Bert was the only one of us to be passed over. I wondered if somebody on the Selection Committee had heard about his "burnt offering".

I love Scotland and being Scottish is something of which I am very proud. That was why at Celtic's first big centenary function in Glasgow I surprised some by wearing a McNeill tartan kilt. There's quite a bit of blue in it! As a player, beating England was the ultimate. So losing to them in my first international was hard to take for one so passionate. It was soul-destroying. The luckiest in our after-match group was my Celtic team-mate Dunky MacKay. He was twelfth man and was glad he hadn't been in at the kick-off.

We became the butt of jokes. The Wembley ball was orange-coloured and it was said that Frank Haffey wouldn't catch it and Eric Caldow and Bobby Shearer refused to kick it. It sounds funny now but not at the time. St. John was as sick as me. It didn't help when Pat Quinn pointed out that "The Saint" couldn't have played

Happy times with a Scotland squad which included Denis Law, Jim Baxter and Ian Ure.

too badly as the England centre-half, Peter Swan, hadn't scored!

I remember, too, Denis Law clobbering Bobby Robson, now the England manager, in front of the Royal Box. Law was another patriot. He had to live with all the kidding of English players during the season and he didn't like it. I've seldom felt so low. It was my first lesson on how cruel sport can be.

Talking of fervency and loyalty, the fans have these admirable qualities much more than the competitors. Working people always hope that their offspring will become directly involved in making it to the top of the sporting platform which so attracts people. It worries me a little that, because of the enormous sums of money involved nowadays for leading players, they might lose the common touch and create a gulf between themselves and the spectators.

Most players, however, are aware of the importance of a close link with the fans. Behind the scenes they do a lot of unpublicised work. Every week I go to the dressing-room with lists of requests from the fans and the players are pleased to co-operate. This is not confined to Celtic. It happens everywhere. At Ibrox, Tynecastle, Pittodrie, Tannadice, Easter Road and, I have no doubt, even at places like Stranraer. Every day dozens of footballers go to hospitals on cheer-up missions.

Football is no longer merely a matter of going on to the pitch and trying to score goals and earning wages. We in the game have to be aware of where the revenue comes from and players have a responsibility to stimulate interest. The game is concerned with training, resting, preparing, meeting fans, visiting hospitals and public relations. Only a small percentage of players abuse their position. None under my control would be allowed to do so for long. I have standards which I expect to be maintained — or else! It is the only way to be successful.

Anyway, the week after that Wembley debacle we met Dunfermline in the Cup final at Hampden, where Jock Stein was to feature prominently again — as manager of the opposition! He had moved to East End Park to gain management experience and this match was to mark the first of many great managerial triumphs for him.

Denis Connachan, the Dunfermline 'keeper, had a spectacular game in a goalless draw seen by 113,328 and, in the Wednesday replay, they went on to beat us 2-0. The Stein influence had brought the Cup to Dunfermline who had never previously even reached the semi-final stage. They say it is no loss what a friend gets but I didn't really feel that way. This defeat, coupled with my first Wembley experience, simply underlined that football is loaded with highs and lows.

51

Chapter Three

The Big Man

IF Jock Stein hadn't returned to Celtic in March 1965, I hate to think what might have happened to the club. It could have taken a nosedive. He certainly averted, quite brilliantly, a severe decline when he took over from Jimmy McGrory, who became the club PRO after being manager for nearly 20 years. The Big Man went on to take Celtic to heights that even he could not have thought possible.

We finished up that season by winning the Scottish Cup, our first major trophy in seven years, and, ironically, it was against Dunfermline, who had beaten us so dramatically four years before. It was my special pleasure to head the winner as we twice fought back, with Bertie Auld scoring two.

Perhaps we would have won that Hampden victory anyway, I don't know, but in the Big Man's first League match on his return, 10 March 1965, we beat Airdrie 6-0 and Bertie Auld scored five. Bertie was Jimmy McGrory's last signing, from Birmingham City, before he stepped down, but I have a feeling Stein was consulted about the move even though he was then with Hibs. Many Hibs fans thought at the time that if Stein had stayed a little longer in Edinburgh Hibs, and not Willie Waddell's Kilmarnock, would have won the League.

By this time Celtic had slipped to eighth place in the championship, not the kind of form acceptable to our supporters, and we also lost to Rangers in the League Cup final during a spell when I missed three months of action due to injury.

In the next season Celtic won the title, the League Cup and were

Learning from the immortals, Jock Stein and Bill Shankly. The picture was taken in August 1974, before my testimonial game against Liverpool.

runners-up in the Scottish Cup (Kai Johansen scored the winner for Rangers in a replay after a goalless draw) as well as semi-finalists in the Cup Winners' Cup in which we beat Liverpool 1-0 at Parkhead but conceded two goals in the return leg. Then on to season 1966-67 in which Celtic swept to victory in every competition, including the European Cup and the domestic treble. We won the championship by three points from Rangers and completed the double over 11 of the 17 other clubs in the old First Division. Celtic lost only two matches in that Stein-inspired, superb season and both were to Dundee United.

Under the Big Man's guidance Celtic won a remarkable 25 trophies. The European Cup, the first-ever British victory, took precedence. But he also led us to ten championship wins (including a world record-equalling nine in a row), eight Scottish Cup final triumphs and six League Cup final victories. Celtic's

League record in the historic Stein era was: played 421, won 296, drawn 66, lost 59, with 1,111 goals scored and only 413 conceded.

What was the special magic, the untold secret, the unique talent of this one-time Lanarkshire miner who was told by the late Bill Shankly, of Liverpool, at the end of our great night in Lisbon against a shocked Inter Milan: "Jock, you're immortal"?

I personally felt an incredible void when he left Parkhead's coaching staff to go to Dunfermline. He was a friend. I couldn't call him a father figure at that time because he was too young. I kept in touch with him during his stay at East End Park and then when he moved on to Hibs. I think he saw in me somebody who was very much like himself apart, of course, from being a centre-half as he had been.

To be honest, in the 1964-65 season I felt that my career didn't seem to be going in any definite direction, and I had made up my mind that it was time to move on at the age of 25 as I couldn't see anything positive happening at the club. Then, with no warning, I was told Big Jock was coming back to Celtic. I remember phoning him to say how pleased I was.

Immediately training altered dramatically. None of the humdrum running round the track as if we were preparing for a marathon. I remember him taking us to the Inverclyde Centre at Largs, and all of a sudden we were doing shooting exercises and everyone was practising with a ball. This hadn't happened before. Training took on a completely new dimension. We loved it. It was a pleasure to come to the Park every day.

All of a sudden any reason, any thought, any suggestion of leaving Celtic simply evaporated. Apart from his knowledge and personality Big Jock was never complicated about anything he asked you to do. I remember players who had been with other clubs, maybe with more sophisticated coaches, thinking it was all too simple. It was simple — the basics. He never asked people to do things they weren't capable of doing. He also recognised when he came to Parkhead that he had a very talented group of people with whom to work. He merely influenced them and introduced confidence. Players were required to do things they enjoyed and the whole scene just opened up like a flower in bloom.

In addition to this he made very shrewd acquisitions in Joe McBride and Willie Wallace. He saw them as being essential to

This was me in action just before I announced my retiral. The game was the Scottish Cup final against Airdrie on 3 May 1975. We won 3-1.

enhance what he had. As I was captain Big Jock often confided in me and it was his intention to team McBride and Wallace but, unfortunately, Joe was injured in our Lisbon year after scoring 18 goals in 14 matches. Steve Chalmers moved in very successfully to replace him and he ended the season as top scorer with 23 as well as getting the winner in the European Cup final. Nevertheless, McBride and Wallace were two great buys. What a goalscorer Joe was and how unlucky to be hurt at such a crucial time. He wasn't the most classy or stylish centre-forward but he was totally effective, with an explosive finish.

My personal situation was difficult. Leaving Celtic would have been terrible but I still had some very good offers to do so. I know that 'tapping' is illegal but it goes on. Spurs were interested in me and I got the tom-toms that Manchester United wanted me to join Paddy Crerand at Old Trafford. Leeds United were also sniffing around. Only the Stein influence kept me with Celtic and I have never had any reason to regret it.

What can I regret in my life as a player? Nine championships in a row plus the European Cup. I used to waken up in the morning and say to myself, "Great, I'm going into training today." Big Jock had that effect on us. The biggest thing he did was to wipe out boredom.

There was always something when Big Jock was around. He was a noisy big so-and-so. And he was nosey, too. He was a wind-up specialist and he found out about everything. These were things that kept players on edge with him. He would walk into a room and hit a player with something and leave him wondering how on earth he had found out an item of information which was being kept under wraps. He had his spies everywhere.

He was always poking fun at us. He had a talent for recognising people's strengths and weaknesses. He would probe at the weaknesses so that it was his victim who became embarrassed. I remember when he was coach of the reserves he used to challenge players to a "fight" over the treatment table. You had to put a foot under the table and were allowed to move its length. The idea was to slap each other. But Big Jock had hands like shovels — he used to skelp us. But really all he was trying to do was get a bit of a laugh. He battered us, but it was in fun and that's the way all of us took it. I remember coming away from Parkhead with big red weals on my body. But, believe me, it was his way of having a diversion to routine. It was like the man himself — outrageous.

This was the manager who transformed a club with a proud tradition and a proud background into a club with a proud present and future and gave it a reputation it would never have approached without him. He was so ambitious, so successful and so good at public relations. He was also a lucky man. Luck was a paramount part of his existence. But isn't this true of all men right at the top of their profession?

The commonsense approach to any problem was his style. Sean Fallon was the assistant manager for most of the time under Big Jock, but another important man was Neilly Mochan. Stein had an outgoing personality, Fallon was the rough, tough guy. But Neilly was a quiet man who counselled players behind the scenes, advised them when they had gone too far, told them when it was more prudent to stay quiet. Neilly also had a great idea and knowledge of football and Big Jock recognised this.

The team that won the European Cup was an extravagant outfit. All were totally different and could be outrageous personalities. We trained hard, worked hard, and played hard. Away from things when we got a chance to enjoy ourselves we could get very close to going over the top. Getting us back to reality was Neilly's department. Neilly would tell us we'd gone too far and that Big Jock was ready to explode. And when he did . . . well . . . ahem . . . what a temper he had. He didn't miss us. I've seen him pinning Willie Wallace behind a bedroom door. I was in the room as well so I knew I would be the next to get it. Unless you could get out of his way — and this was possible because his injured ankle made him a bit immobile — he would hit out.

Big Jock liked to have the reputation of being big and hard. But he wasn't really. There was another side to him altogether. He could be quiet and compassionate, which was a lovely touch with his players. Although at times he rode over us roughshod there was his other side which could be nice and soft. He was the best manager of his time by the width of the Clyde at Gourock.

In those days there was no freedom of contract. To leave a club was difficult. It wasn't merely a case of going at the end of a contract. The contract was for life. Big Jock knew how best to capitalise on this and, as I have said, he also bought shrewdly on the transfer market. £30,000 for Willie Wallace from Hearts was a fortune in December 1966. Joe McBride cost £20,000 from Motherwell. It was good business, though.

Tactically, Big Jock didn't go daft by being hard and rigid. He was always full of ideas, though. In the main he was excellent at sizing up the opposition, which was especially important to us as we didn't have the advantage of seeing so many of the Continental teams on TV. We trained on our own strengths and didn't go overboard about the opposition.

Big Jock was great at asking his players to do what they were best at. He rarely misjudged the talent of his staff. He knew their capabilities and didn't confuse the issue by asking any of us to do what we found difficult. Our planning was within a framework but he always looked for improvisation and we had the kind of team that could respond to that. Often against Rangers, for instance, we would play with two deep-lying wide players to pull out their full-backs so that we could then play into the channels behind them. Big Jock wasn't too much of a blackboard man but often before European ties we would discuss the use of overlapping full-backs, with the idea of Tommy Gemmell getting to their penalty box, Bobby Lennox making cross-runs and so on.

Like Big Jock I believe the apex of a defence is the strongest part so the idea is to get behind it from the flanks. This was his plan in Lisbon. I support the idea of wide players, but nowadays the game has altered so much that the recognised winger is hard to incorporate into modern-day football. However, if the width of the park isn't utilised then the bit in the middle becomes very difficult.

He never assessed opponents for big European ties until after the Saturday game was out of the way. Then he would start, perhaps at Seamill, and would spend maybe half an hour telling us how the opposition set themselves out. Then he would suggest the type of things we should do to combat them. Mind you, we didn't need an awful lot of pointing in any direction because of the team's experience.

When I first returned to Parkhead, as manager, in May 1978, Jock Stein was offered a directorship. He had been instrumental in arranging my return. My friends in the Press will be surprised to find out that the first 'feelers' were put out under their very noses — at the Scottish Football Writers' dinner in Glasgow, in fact. I had

Sean Fallon puts me through my paces.

come down from Aberdeen where I was happy and settled. All of a sudden Big Jock asked me if I would like to return to Paradise.

My heart would never have let me go anywhere else but I often wonder what my head would have done. Having returned to Glasgow I got the impression that I was almost manipulated into it. The news slipped out while I was presenting prizes at Stonehaven and District Primary Schools final which wasn't the best time to be asked if I was leaving Aberdeen. The story appeared in the *Evening Times*, which took me by surprise. I had no idea anybody outside of a small circle could be aware of an approach to me as it had been informal.

I spoke to Big Jock again after another sportsmen's function at the MacDonald Hotel in Giffnock. We shot along Eastwood Mains Road into Davieland Road and sat talking about it for a couple of hours in his Mercedes. He told me he was moving out of management into a board position which, in fact, he didn't accept. Then his testimonial match came and all of a sudden he was away to Leeds.

I talked to him about staying at Parkhead, but I could tell by the way he wasn't being forthcoming that there was something else in the wind. Was it the Scottish job? He certainly came back from Leeds, which I didn't think was right for him, to take over at the SFA very quickly. I felt he should have accepted the Scotland job long before he did. It was offered to him on 7 June 1975, but he opted to stay with Celtic. At the same time, I would have been delighted if he had agreed to stay on with Celtic when I became manager.

I had offered my services to Big Jock after he had a very bad car accident near Dumfries while on the way home from holiday. I knew all kinds of things were happening. Davie McParland was made an assistant manager and Sean Fallon was moved to chief scout. I asked Big Jock to appoint me as an assistant but he was non-committal. The relationship between us was never quite the same when I quit playing after helping Celtic to beat Airdrie 3-1 in the Scottish Cup final on 3 May 1975. I had played 832 games for the club.

I had the feeling when I spoke to the Big Man about returning to help him that things weren't totally in his control. It was a disappointment that I couldn't have assisted him at that important stage when he was getting over the accident and, before that, a mild heart attack.

When Big Jock *did* take over Scotland he promised to involve me. I was with Celtic then but it would have been invaluable experience for me. He told several others the same thing, including Benny Rooney. His plan, he said, was to involve lots of managers with the full international team and the under-21's. I've always regretted that he didn't follow this up. He never told me why.

The car accident and the heart trouble before it took a lot out of Jock Stein. I looked at him and felt that something had gone from his bubbling personality. Perhaps he asked too much even of himself. I certainly thought he should have relaxed an awful lot more than he did.

Maybe I'm wrong, but I thought a wee drink now and again would have done him good. He was a teetotaller, though, and didn't care to get relaxation in this way. I looked at Big Jock, Bill Shankly and Sir Matt Busby who were contempories. The Shanks, like Big Jock, had all this pent-up energy but didn't drink. Sir Matt is still going strong and he likes the odd drink. Having moved into management, I certainly find it's necessary to have the opportunity to relax. Big Jock liked horse-racing and he had a dabble at bowling. But I didn't think that was enough to take his mind fully off work.

Jock Stein died at work, watching his Scotland team playing in a World Cup-tie at Wales which qualified them to play-off successfully against Australia. The whole of the football world mourned him and, at Celtic Park, most of us feel his epitaph is the club itself. He took Celtic to heights only dreamed of and it is appropriate to remember this in the club's centenary year.

Chapter Four

The Lisbon Lions

AMONG the most marvellous things about football are the memories of great games, and none could possibly be better than Celtic's 90-minute duel in the sun with Internationale Milan in the Estadio Nacional in Lisbon, on 25 May 1967.

Celtic became the first British team to win the European Cup and I, as the team captain, had to stand like Caesar on the Forum to accept the trophy. What we had done, what we had achieved and what a surprise our 2-1 victory aroused around Europe didn't really hit us until we returned to Glasgow and saw people lining the streets all the way from the old Renfrew Airport. I know that Liverpool have won the trophy three times since then, Nottingham Forest twice and Manchester United and Aston Villa once each. But Celtic were the pathfinders, against an Italian team reckoned to be invincible. The teams are worth recalling: *Celtic*: Simpson, Craig, Gemmell, Murdoch, McNeill, Clark, Johnstone, Wallace, Chalmers, Auld, Lennox. *Inter Milan*: Sarti, Burgnich, Facchetti, Bedin, Guarneri, Picchi, Domenghini, Cappellini, Mazzola, Bicicli, Corso.

The chief thing on our side was that it was a one-off match. It was our first time in the European Champions Cup and we were in the final right away. The weather was warm, but not uncomfortably so. We were based at the superb Palaccio Hotel in Estoril. We felt really at home because there were hundreds of Celtic fans around and the Portuguese seemed to be on our side as well.

In fact, we were almost jealous of the supporters who were so obviously having a ball. They had left Scotland by all kinds of

Heading for Europe.

means, including a car cavalcade. Some fans even hitched to and from Lisbon and there were queues at the British Consul the morning after the match asking to be given help to get home. It may well be apocryphal, but I was told a good story later about a fan, green and white from head to foot and well refreshed, who was offered a lift in an Edinburgh-bound car just outside Lisbon. He thanked the driver politely but said the offer was no good as he came from Wishaw.

Our preparations in the sunshine were great. On the second day the Italians were supposed to train after us, but they reversed this so that they could watch us limbering up. What they could learn

63

from looking on at a training session I can't imagine. But Jock Stein used this to fire us up. He called them cheats and went on to us about their underhand methods. He was using the situation to stir us up. It was good management.

Before the match Helenio Herrera, the Inter manager, tried another tactic to upset us. He went to the bench allocated to us and said he intended to stay there. Sean Fallon had a word with him and pointed out the folly of such an action if our manager got really riled.

Our preparation on the eve of the game would astonish many modern players. A Scot, Brodie Lennox, had a golfing country club in Estoril and he invited us to his house to watch the televised match between England and Spain. Then we walked back, led by Neilly Mochan whose walks were famous for the tortuous routes he took. We ended up climbing over fences and crawling through undergrowth to get to our hotel. I thought to myself, "What a preparation for a European Cup final." It was astonishing how relaxed we were. The game was to be beamed live throughout Europe and to many other parts of the world and here we were, the novices in the eyes of our Italian opponents, treating the occasion as if it was just another match on foreign territory.

The best thing that happened to us was losing a penalty goal after only seven minutes. Jim Craig, chasing Cappellini across the penalty area, was adjudged to have fouled him but it didn't look a foul to us. We felt really aggrieved and thought that the West German referee Kurt Tschescher had done us in. At half-time we were blazing and wanted to have a go at the referee. The mood didn't displease Jock Stein. Angry Scots try even harder, particularly if they think there has been an injustice. There had been none as it turned out. Having watched the incident a million times on video the decision was technically correct. Mazzola scored from the kick and sent Ronnie Simpson diving the wrong way.

We had thought the weak link in Inter's defence would be the goalkeeper Sarti. He was their hero. But for his brilliance Inter would have been thrashed. This wouldn't have been an unpopular outcome as Inter's brand of defensive play was hated by supporters, including their own.

What made the game even more dramatic was that we had to wait for such a long time before making a breakthrough. For nearly

Hail, hail the fans are here — and we had just won our seventh League flag in a row.

an hour all Celtic's efforts were beaten off. We scored in 62 minutes. Bobby Murdoch passed to Jim Craig, who cut the ball back to Tommy Gemmell on the fringe of the penalty area. His great shot zoomed into the top right hand corner of Sarti's goal.

The winner came with only five minutes to go and was scored by Steve Chalmers. Bobby Murdoch shot low across the goal and Chalmers stuck out a foot to score the most important goal of any Scot in a club game before or since.

This was easily the best team I was privileged to play in. There are only a few others whom I've teamed up with at Parkhead who would have been good enough to get a place in it. The nice thing about the Lisbon Lions team, as we became known, is that we haven't lost an affinity with each other. Looking back it's unfortunate that some of the lads who didn't play in the final but nevertheless made a contribution in that season — such as Charlie Gallagher, Joe McBride, John Hughes, Ian Young, Willie O'Neill and John Fallon — were just left on the edge of things. It's always that eleven who are talked about as the Lions. I often feel sorry for these players.

There is a general belief, by the way, that I got the nickname Caesar after standing up in the Lisbon stand to get the trophy. This is not so. A group of us jokingly formed outselves into a Sinatra-style 'rat pack'. I was nicknamed Caesar Romero because I was the only one with a car at the time!

It was a great feeling being up there to take the Cup but, annoyingly, I didn't have a team to go back to on the pitch. The crowd invaded the park, though it was all very friendly. There was no chance of anyone being hurt. However, my team-mates were taken to the dressing-room instead of standing at the edge of the pitch while I got the trophy. I walked through the crowd to get there but was taken round the stadium in a police car on the way back.

When people talk of pitch invasions nowadays it means a serious interruption but this wasn't the case in Lisbon. The supporters were wandering about in sheer delight. When I look at the video of *The Celtic Story* I know a lot of the fellows who were on the pitch, including one wearing a kilt. Without knowing their names I feel I know them well.

I had swopped jerseys with one of the Italians but that disappeared. Everything, in fact, went but we didn't really care. As we were travelling into Lisbon for the medal presentation which should have taken place on the pitch, Portuguese supporters were driving past us laughing and waving strips and boots which had been ours some short time before! Anything that was lying about was nicked. It was fair game for souvenir hunters.

In fact, the final was the easiest game we defenders had had in Europe during that year. It was frustrating. After they scored we put Inter under such pressure they never managed even to threaten us. Early in the game Ronnie Simpson came out and backheeled the ball away. Only he could have got away with that — his best saves were often made in a most unusual fashion. But he was the most frustrating 'keeper to play against.

John Clark and I were like a couple of extras, we had so little to do. The full-backs got involved in forward runs, of course, but all we did was get the ball and pass it to one of the others. The boys up front and the midfield really played well. They had good-quality shots at goal and wee Jimmy Johnstone hit the bar twice. There was a spell when we couldn't understand why we weren't scoring goals. It was frightening. I had a chance myself, when I went up for a free kick, but I jumped on the wrong side of the defender. If I had gone the other way I would certainly have scored. Every time I look at the film I think what an idiot I was.

What a reception when we got back to Glasgow! It was then that what we'd done began to sink in. There was a fabulous turn-out at Celtic Park. I felt nearly overwhelmed. I think we all looked the part. But this might not have been so had Ronnie Simpson not remembered to pick his cap out of the back of the net in Lisbon as fans hunted for souvenirs. You see, some of the players put their false teeth in Ronnie's bunnet for safe-keeping during the game. Imagine if some of us had attended the celebrations minus our front molars.

It's amazing the impact we still have when we get together as a group. Twenty years after the big game we assembled for a few days and had a ball, including doing a programme for Scottish Television from Seamill. I wondered if the bond would still be as strong. It is, despite the fact that we are all complex and most are strong characters.

Ronnie Simpson — and I'm sure he'll appreciate this ! — was almost a father figure. He was the guy in the team with whom any one of us could have at least a semi-serious conversation at any time. He is a naturally funny person, with the bulk of his jokes aimed at himself. Nobody could fall out with him. He is one of the most affable blokes you could meet. If we lost a goal Ronnie would point accusingly at various defenders, then throw up his arms and shout: "Okay, it's my fault again!" He was naturally droll and really enjoyed his football career which really took off so dramatically late, after his move to Parkhead from Hibs.

Dentist Jim Craig was the unusual member of the side. We kidded that if there was athletics across the road and a football match in front of him he would watch the runners. We called him the "Happy Amateur", mostly because he had been at Glasgow University and Dental College. I think "Cairney" came into football as an afterthought, whereas most of the others had devoted their lives entirely to the game. Stable, straightforward and sensible, he always looked on the more serious side.

Tommy Gemmell's outgoing personality was vital and it made him larger than life. He imposed his personality on every winger in

The glorious Lisbon Lions — 20 years on. Standing: Craig, Gemmell, McNeill,
Simpson, Murdoch, Clark.
Kneeling: Johnstone, Wallace, Chalmers, Auld, Lennox.

the world — or, at least, the ones who came up against him. He
didn't worry about wingers. He left all that to them. I remember in
a Miami hotel Tommy entered a talent competition. When the
Yanks saw him, they shouted: "Gee . . . there's Danny Kaye."
That was all Tommy needed. He proceeded to put on a show of
which the great Danny might well have been proud.

On the right side of the half-back line Bobby Murdoch, who
went to the same school as me, was the cog of the side. In these
days we had two wing-halves. Bobby was one and Bertie Auld
basically the other. Bobby was a superb passer of the ball, a good
finisher and very determined in everything — in fact, a good all-
rounder and very much in the Paul McStay mould. For a big fellow
he had exceptional vision. Off the field he was much quieter than
his presence on it may have suggested.

John Clark, who later became my assistant manager, was a
serious type as a player. He read every football magazine ever
printed and knew about all the leading foreign teams. I roomed

with John regularly and he could be good fun. He was an important member of the side and very dependable. I always felt he was a steadier person than most of the others.

Up front the number one was Jimmy Johnstone. Wee "Jinky" is one of the most sparkling people I've met. In fact, had he been able to control the whole thing he could have been the best TV personality this country has seen. I'm not just talking about football. He can sing well and is a smashing joke-teller. When he impersonated Rod Stewart I thought he was better than the real thing! Jimmy was an entertainer, a very productive one at that. He was so talented as a player he found it hard to conform to a team pattern. The rest of us could cope with this and knew when things were right for Jimmy. Celtic and Jimmy were perfect for each other.

Willie Wallace, whom I talk to regularly by phone in Australia, was mischievous. He invariably had a smile on his face and a twinkle in his eye. "Wispy" — so called because of his throaty whisper — was the boy next door with that wee bit of devil. He could play in a variety of positions. I was pleased when he was signed from Hearts although I remembered him before that with Raith Rovers. He was quiet, good fun and was always ready with a prank.

Our centre-forward, Stevie Chalmers, later became a wee bit of an elder statesman. We kidded that he was the same age as Ronnie Simpson. Stevie hardly changed in appearance the whole time he played and still looks great as a member of the club pools staff. He was so full of running and determination on the pitch that he was a foil for us all. What he lacked in skill he balanced with enterprise and running-power. A very stable sort of guy with a confident way, he enjoyed the laughs with us, although he was never an instigator.

Bertie Auld is a lovable rogue with a sharp personality and super wit. He came away with quips we wished we had thought of ourselves. He has a rapid-fire tongue. Once, in a game with Leeds at Parkhead, he had been tackling very hard. Coming out for the second half Johnny Giles warned that hard man Norman Hunter would be after him in the second half. To which Bertie replied: "Oh, good, I hope he's a white hunter!" Bertie liked us to get a grip of a game early so that he could then take over with his delightful passes and showmanship. He switched from being a conventional hard-running winger to a very skilful midfield prompter. Bertie once sat on the ball during a game and I don't think Jock Stein ever forgave him.

Bobby Lennox was a foil for everybody. He is a smashing outgoing personality, friendly and full of fun. As a player, when some prank was going on Bobby was usually involved. On the pitch he had tremendous running power and was a great scorer. A nice guy who always said he wasn't brave but was certainly never frightened in a game.

I believe a player's character is very important in the make-up of a successful team. If players don't want to mix there is a problem. There's a fine line between eccentric behaviour and indiscipline. Within a team players must look after each other. I did a lot of that as the captain but Ronnie Simpson, Jim Craig, Stevie Chalmers and John Clark also helped a lot.

The strength of what Celtic call "The Good Team" was that we could laugh, argue and fight — sometimes to extremes — but always remained a team who would not let outsiders criticise a colleague. Frankly we did quite a lot to extremes . . . played hard, trained hard, and enjoyed ourselves thoroughly. I compared us to the old Labour Party which, in the privacy of its own ranks, could argue, dispute and fall out. But to the outside world we always showed a united front.

I have already mentioned players who were on the fringe of the Lions and one or two by sheer misfortune because they might well have been in the final at Lisbon. Joe McBride was KO'd by injury, for instance. He is a happy-go-lucky personality, but was a tremendous striker of the ball and a fine scorer. Players such as Joe and John Hughes came to Celtic Park not knowing whether they would play on a Saturday or not. Jock Stein would talk of "freshening up" and that meant moving a couple of forwards out and in. "Yogi" was big and fit — a powerhouse — and for one so massive he had tremendous ability, although he was unpredictable.

In Charlie Gallagher's case he was so classy that some wondered if he should have been in instead of Bertie Auld. Charlie was a super passer with considerable ability on the ball. He didn't have Bertie's outgoing personality but he was still a good prompter.

Ian Young seemed very nearly to disappear from the scene, but in the early days of our development he played a very prominent

Up and down — I head for goal against Dunfermline in season 1971-72.

part. Willie O'Neill would have broken through but for the fact that the left-back was Tommy Gemmell. Jim Brogan also started to come into things. John Fallon was the eternal reserve goalie. I could never understand why he was so pally with Ronnie Simpson, although I've seen this comradeship between first and second string keepers before. Privately, I thought that in the same situation I might have put a pillow over my rival's head in his sleep. John Cushley, who stood in for me from time to time, never took his chance!

I doubt if any team, before or since, has ever trained harder than the players of the Lions era. But we also enjoyed ourselves. The bond between us will never be broken. I see great similarities between the present team and the Lions in the early days. The next step is obviously going to be important. We must see how Celtic go from here. A difficulty nowadays is keeping a side together because of freedom of contract. The system has my wholehearted support as players are entitled to decide their own destiny like everyone else. But it does present problems for ambitious clubs with long-term plans.

Enjoyment, and not money, was the Lions' motivator although we did go round the world. We were in Bermuda three times, for instance. Football was played with great smiles and spectators enjoyed games in similar style. I wonder if time has caught up with us. It is so much more difficult to reproduce that kind of atmosphere.

I've looked hard at subsequent Celtic players who could have forced themselves into the Lions side and come up with only Kenny Dalglish, Danny McGrain, George Connelly and, undoubtedly, Paul McStay.

We were very much a unit and the players never ever thought they were the only people who were important. Jock Stein was obviously a key figure but there were also Sean Fallon, Neilly Mochan, Bob Rooney and Jim Steele. Each played an important part. "Steely" is really something else! I've never met a man who is liked by so many people. He's marvellous. I find it difficult to be specific about his contribution to Celtic, but over more than 40 years he has provided fun, noise and non-stop activity for Celtic players — as well as livening up muscles with his massages.

"Steely" trained one-time world light-heavyweight champion Freddie Mills when he was a PT instructor in the RAF. He looked after Mills for around three years. It was Tommy Docherty who first recruited "Steely" to Scotland's international set-up and every manager since has used him, including Andy Roxburgh. He has never taken a penny from Celtic. Being a part of the set-up is payment enough for him. I am delighted to be able to call "Steely" a friend and I know so many current and past players who feel the same way. For "Steely" life is a ball. I've never seen him in a bad mood and I doubt if he even knows the feeling. He is also one of these remarkable people who isn't bothered by language difficulties. He seems to be international.

Bob Rooney was one of the old-fashioned physios, a combination of trainer and physio. Bob involved himself a lot in the training. He also used a bit of psychology with injured players, having been a professional himself. Sean Fallon was important behind the scenes as Big Jock's lieutenant and Neilly Mochan played a vital role too.

My last word on the Lions is that though we played hard off the pitch, we also trained harder to be good on it. If we had a night out the players knew we had to work damned hard in the morning at training. More than once Jock Stein acknowledged to me as captain that he couldn't begin to fault us in the important area of attitude.

Chapter Five

My Big Cash Crash

WHEN I stopped playing, at 35, my plan was to carve out a new future in the business world. In the end I was very nearly ruined. I lost an estimated £85,000 and had to sell my family home at Pollokshields in Glasgow to give my bankbook some stability again.

There is a very good pension scheme into which players can pay and, by the age at which I retired, they can be very nicely set up. I elected to put all my cash into a company called Milnrow Development in the belief that it would secure my future. The company crashed and I lost nearly everything I had put away for the future. It was a personal disaster. My wife, Liz, was remarkably philosophical about the loss of our nest-egg. I think women are better at accepting these situations. The fact that Liz took it all in her stride really helped me to work at a recovery.

An accountant, Frank McCormack, and my former team-mate Joe McBride, were my co-directors. They both argued it was time for me to get out of football to concentrate on the business. I felt that by then I wasn't as good a player. It is a fact of life that the older you get the less athletic you become. Experience, and the know-how it creates, was carrying me along. I had also distanced myself from most of the other players. The ones with whom I grew up had mostly gone.

Yet I regretted retiring when I did almost as soon as I made the announcement, but didn't feel I could go back on it. Playing football was a way of life. I sometimes even put Celtic ahead of my family. There is an attraction about stopping at the top, but in many ways the end product is hollow. I could have played on enjoyably, instead of putting myself in the position of starting all over again so abruptly. Becoming involved in the company on a full-time basis was the biggest influence in making my decision. I had no thoughts then of becoming a manager. The future I envisaged was not in football.

A tag which had begun to annoy me was "veteran". The use of this word in the papers to describe me towards the end of my playing career was upsetting. I have given experienced players advice about when to retire and I always say the end of the season is not the time to make a decision. It is understandable that players feel tired at the end of a season. It happens to youngsters, too. So the thing to do is wait for a few months and judge how you feel when it comes to September or October. Making a decision in haste can be bad.

Obviously, nobody can go on playing for ever. Ideally, though, there should be a phasing-out period. The experience that I had gained at a very high level could have been beneficial to other clubs. And I could have had some fun in the process. Football is all about enjoyment — for the players and the people who come to watch. In retrospect I still had a contribution to make on the pitch when I decided instead to retire. I could have gone on to 38 or 40.

Liz and I had just returned to Southampton from a cruise in the Mediterranean when we heard about Jock Stein's car accident. We had planned to live for a week with friends in Woking, Surrey, but stayed only one night and drove to Dumfries to see Big Jock in hospital.

I realised he would need a fair period of recovery. In these unexpected circumstances I thought the club might have asked me to play on, but they never ever did. Perhaps I should have taken the initiative and offered my services. However, Johannes Edvaldsson had come to the club and Roddie MacDonald was being given his head, so Celtic probably thought it was better to make a fresh start. It was obvious they had to rebuild.

At that particular time, in 1975, I was offered the managership of Ayr United. I really wanted to take the job because I felt it was a club with potential at a ground where I had always enjoyed matches. The Ayr job was made more attractive to me by the fact that a lot of Milnrow's interests were in Ayrshire and I felt I could have coped. Ayr would have been happy for me to do both jobs, but after talking to Frank and Joe I considered it more important for me to concentrate fully on the business. I often look back and think how the experience of running Ayr United might have helped me greatly.

When I quit I also had the chance to join the NASL which had just started in Canada and America. I received a remarkable offer from Vancouver Whitecaps to fly out. They offered me all sorts of inducements. They played Rangers in a tour game and wanted me to turn out against them. That's another thing I regret. I should have taken my family to give them a look at life in another country. It would also have been exciting to be in on the birth of something new in the game.

I should make it clear that I made a net £25,000 from my testimonial match. I've seen a variety of figures quoted, going as high as £60,000. The bulk of the £25,000 went into Milnrow and I made a good capital profit on selling a small pub which I had in Bellshill. This and other monies I had saved all went into the company.

In business we were unlucky. We hit a time when financing became very difficult. Interest charges went through the roof and it was hard enough for big companies. We began by buying properties and renovating them for later sale. Then we hit on the idea of retaining them and renting out. We were doing well, but when Rent Tribunals came along we felt it was a business which had been tarnished. We didn't want to be involved in anything like this, so we sold off the flats and moved into the licensed trade.

Perhaps we were too adventurous. We had hotels at Strathaven, Fenwick, Coylton and Torranyard. But it became apparent because of high interest rates that the company couldn't afford too many full-time executives. This coincided with me moving into football management at Shawfield.

While with Clyde, I had intended to buy a small pub to supplement my income but, out of the blue, came the offer to join Aberdeen as manager. I resigned as a company director just before going to Pittodrie. The Milnrow company then changed quite dramatically because they bought the Lomond Castle Hotel at Balloch, and the development of this and the Torranyard as a caravan site may have been over-ambitious. Subsequently, the

Carefree days as a player and captain.

whole thing went to the wall. I had tried to get my money out but this proved to be impossible.

When I came back to Parkhead from Aberdeen it was very obvious the company had serious problems. At one point I agreed to buy the hotel at Strathaven — Liz and I had even thought about building a house there — but this would have meant me borrowing and leaving what I had invested in Milnrow. At the end of the day I didn't go through with the deal.

It was a very trying experience. All of a sudden the 18 years I had spent playing football didn't mean a thing. I was lucky that I had another job. But the whole thing affected me more than Liz. She coped with all the worries remarkably. I had to sell our house although I held on as long as I could. It was ironical that, although we bought another one near Rouken Glen, we were on the move again to Manchester within six weeks.

This fact surely illustrates how unprepared I was for what happened in that close season. We bought the bungalow at the end of April and in June I was on my way from Parkhead. The new house wasn't as good as the one we had in Pollokshields but it was very nice nevertheless. I was just beginning to enjoy living in it when we were uprooted again. Quite a few people seemed to think I had some advance knowledge long before I went to Manchester City, but how could this be so? Surely I wouldn't have been buying a new house.

This brings a point to mind. When Liz and I were married in 1963 we got no advice from any source about how to buy property. I came from a council house background and Liz's father worked in the shipyards. My dad, as I've told you, was a professional soldier, and when he came out of the Army he worked at Ravenscraig. My grandfather was a miner. So there wasn't really anybody to give us practical advice. Nowadays players are better advised on ways to make their futures in football very much more secure. Their pensions scheme is also excellent.

When I was playing there was no such thing as freedom of contract, so we weren't in a good bargaining position. My first wage, as a part-timer with Celtic, was £7 a week. When I turned professional in 1961, having played as an international, I received £24 a week. A star player in our best days, bearing in mind that we were winning the League and Cups, would be doing handstands if

78

his pay was between £8,000 and £9,000. The £25,000 I got in my testimonial is a good way of giving a comparison. Roy Aitken, Tommy Burns and Davie Provan all received in the region of £100,000 tax free.

The most important aspect in my time was that the clubs had the right to retain players. There was talk of slavery, but this was a pretty extravagant description. Sufficient to say the ball was very much in the court of the clubs. Even if your contract was up you couldn't automatically negotiate a fresh deal elsewhere, as happens now. In some ways players were prisoners for life. The advent of freedom of contract puts them, particularly the good ones, in a very strong position. The sky can be the limit in wage negotiations. Indeed, supporters ask why stars have to go. The answer is that sometimes clubs can't afford to meet the demands. They are lucky young men and I hope they appreciate this.

Players in general today don't have the same respect for their profession, and each other, as we did. I also feel we enjoyed the game an awful lot more. Miguel Munoz, Spain's international manager, said fairly recently that their game was deteriorating because of the extortionate demands that footballers were making. I know what he's saying, but it's a short life and the good players are entitled to bargain as hard as they can just so long as they remember that the game is meant to be enjoyed. It has to be conducted in a way which creates entertainment. It's not all about money. Its very basis is founded on living life and doing something you've always wanted. Players have responsibilities and must carry them out.

I have great admiration for Kevin Keegan. He was the first really to take sponsorship on in a big way. But he never lost sight of the fact that he had a duty to give something in return. Too many want to settle a deal without fulfilling their side of the bargain.

Money should not be the main motivating factor. It never was in the team in which I played. Pride and enjoyment were our spurs. I think the standard 20 years ago was better. Players didn't move to the same degree and there wasn't an unsettling period before contracts come to an end.

Most teams today are giving value for money. I certainly like to think Celtic do so. What worries me is that the current big names, or many of them, think of football as a job. However, the pressures on players today are greater, and I contend that too much of the coaching is of a negative type. There is an over-emphasis on destroying opponents. We have become clever about fitness but too often kill skill.

The attitude of supporters has also changed. They are making too many demands. The lower teams have very little chance of real success. Yet so much is expected of them. Fans also enjoyed themselves more 20 or so years ago. Nowadays too many come not so much to have a good time at games but to antagonise each other. Football is often a window to the world. Crowds, and what happens in football grounds, are really only a trailer to what is happening in life generally. I hate it when special study groups talk about football hooliganism. I don't think it's football hooliganism. It's simply hooliganism of the sort to be found anywhere in our currently unruly society. I feel very strongly about this.

When Feyenoord asked us to play a team as close as possible to the 1970 Celtic European Cup final side, as part of the Dutch club's 75th anniversary celebrations, one of their committee made the point to me that we had seen the best of football in its true sense. He recalled that, before and after the 1970 final, fans mingled and exchanged souvenirs. There was a splendid atmosphere. In all probablity they would have been fighting each other today. That is an essential difference between current fans and those of all my yesterdays.

Chapter Six

Scottish Football Revolution

I WAS surprised when Rangers took the plunge and invested money in players on a scale never before attempted in Scotland. It was outstandingly ambitious though, in the early part of their daring scheme, it looked as though it might not be successful. However, Rangers got themselves sorted out and, apart from the hiccup of losing to Hamilton Accies in the Scottish Cup, they achieved their main target of winning the Premier League championship. Rangers then gave indications to all and sundry that they had no intention of standing still. They wanted to improve even further.

Any manager would like to be in Graeme Souness's position of being able to sign the players who, in his judgment, are the best available. The player who has had the biggest impact is Terry Butcher. England's captain coming to Scotland from Ipswich didn't seem possible. He was tipped to go to either Spurs or Manchester United, which made the move to Rangers all the more remarkable. Chris Woods, deputy to Peter Shilton in Bobby Robson's England set-up, following Butcher was also astonishing.

However, fixing up a player-manager was revolutionary in itself. And going to Italy to take Graeme Souness from Sampdoria, while he was still the Scottish international captain, showed a bit of style. It was a spectacular thing to do and has had its effect at several other clubs. Aberdeen raided in the south, notably for Charlie and Peter Nicholas; Hibs paid Oldham £320,000 for goalkeeper Andy Goram and Hearts spent £500,000 on Dave McPherson and Hugh Burns from Rangers and also dabbled in England, although at the lower end of the market. This season Rangers bought Gary Stevens for £1 million from Everton and Kevin Drinkell for half this amount from Norwich. And look at some of the other key signings: Steve Archibald to Hibs from Barcelona, Theo Snelders and Paul Mason from Holland to Aberdeen, Raphael Meade, ex-Arsenal to Dundee United, Iain Ferguson and Eamonn Bannon to Hearts from Dundee United and, of course, goalies Ian Andrews, ex-Leicester, and Alan Rough, from Orlando Lions, to Celtic. It is splendid to see Scottish clubs investing in good players because they are the people who create the interest and entertainment. For too long Scotland has had to watch some of our best players disappearing to England or abroad.

Rangers forced all clubs to rethink the extent of their investment in players and this, of course, included Celtic. The Old Firm always put pressure on each other. Our fans expect, even demand, that we compete on an even basis.

I came back to Parkhead for a second time as manager on 28 May 1987, which was exactly ten years to the day since I was first given the job. It was an awkward time because it coincided with the way-going of Brian McClair, Mo Johnston Murdo MacLeod and Alan McInally. The two leading front players were the most important of this group. Their value was maybe 60 goals in a season.

In fact, I brought McClair from Motherwell for £90,000, using some of the money we got from Arsenal for Charlie Nicholas to carry out the deal. In his first season Brian scored 23 goals and was the club's top scorer. However, I never had the opportunity to work with him. I was annoyed that I never had this chance because soon after he signed I was off to Manchester City on 30 June 1983. And when I came back in 1987 Brian was preparing to leave for Manchester United.

I tried to keep both McClair and Johnston at Parkhead. I had the feeling Mo Johnston was trying to avoid me as I couldn't raise him by phone. So I went to his home to speak to him on a Friday night. He told me he wanted to stay with Celtic and that he wouldn't do anything without first talking to me, although he admitted a move to the Continent was on the cards. He struck me as being a decent enough bloke — but the next thing I heard was that he had joined Nantes in France.

Rangers' taking Graeme Souness from Sampdoria showed a bit of style.

Bobby Lennox puts a matey armlock on Brian McClair.

On my visit to his house, Mo didn't appear to have anything really lined up and subsequent trips abroad seemed to confirm this.

84

I thought his agent was hawking him all over the place. Don't get me wrong, I understand and accept that every player has the right to choose the club with which he wants to play. What I am saying is that Johnston never gave me, as his new manager, a proper opportunity to speak to him about his future.

McClair was a bigger disappointment. Having taken him from Motherwell originally I thought he owed me something. However, I was aware that it was an open secret in Manchester that Alex Ferguson was very interested in taking McClair to Old Trafford. In fact, Fergie told me himself that McClair was an obvious target for a club like United because he would always score a lot of goals. This view was justified by the fact that in April Brian became the first Old Trafford player since George Best in 1967 to score 20 goals in a season.

I was forced to meet Brian with his agent, who had drawn up a list of items to be discussed. Before we could get started on this I wanted to know what the player really wanted. He told me they were looking for a signing-on fee of £200,000 and a salary of £100,000 a year. I knew, from earlier discusions I had had with our chairman, Jack McGinn, that there wasn't really much point in going on.

The agent, from London, assured me he had two clubs in England who were prepared to pay these figures. I told him his client was a very lucky young man. I suggested they should lock the door behind them in case the clubs changed their minds. The agent persisted and asked me to look at his list. He wanted to set any future transfer fee — and this was in addition to the £200,000. He also asked for mortgage assistance, which I thought was quite funny. Imagine a player getting this kind of signing-on fee and salary and still requiring mortgage assistance!

There were also bonuses for scoring goals and I remember asking what the players who set them up would get. And, indeed, if Brian could be fined for missing. The last item on the sheet illustrated how difficult it can be for a football manager to deal with an agent. He wanted to fix a limit to the number of competitive games that Brian would play. It's interesting that he should put forward such a proposition because I don't see how any club could agree to it.

I am not totally against agents, by the way. I defend any player's right to seek professional advice. Nobody can argue against this. What I feel is that agents do themselves and their clients a disservice when they make unreasonable demands to sign and play, plus daft perks on top. In the main, an agent really only makes money himself when a player moves to another team. So a club trying to hold on to a player at the end of his contract is at a disadvantage.

If we tally up what McClair was offered by Celtic in guaranteed wages and signing-on fees, it was a huge contract which would have made him a very serious contender as Scotland's highest-paid footballer. The Manchester United deal, according to details shown to us at the tribunal, was only minimally better — if at all — and I assume that is the contract on which he is now operating. So I still wonder why Brian was so keen to move south. Outside influences appeared to make it better for him to go. I got the distinct feeling that Brian was merely going through the motions when he spoke to me, so that he could always say he had given the club a fair chance. If we had accepted the unrealistic terms which his agent originally suggested then perhaps — only perhaps — he might have changed his mind. Throughout the discussions Brian seemed completely disinterested and concentrated more on playing with a piece of thread. He ventured only one question which was to ask Jack McGinn if Celtic had ambition.

Clubs such as Celtic must live with the freedom of contract plan and, at the same time, be fair and reasonable. Money alone should never be the reason for players being in the game. I respect their right to earn as much as they can in a comparatively short period, but I would always be annoyed if they put financial gain ahead of the spirit of the sport. I think this is true particularly with clubs such as Celtic, who have demonstrated that those who play the bulk of their careers with us will be well rewarded. We have to look no further than Roy Aitken, Tommy Burns and Davie Provan.

Fans are also entitled to something in return. Too many players have left Celtic, including McClair and Johnston, saying it was very hard to part because the supporters are so good. It's true our fans are special, but what the players say is camouflage and a load of rubbish. They make up their own minds whether to stay or leave, and if the people in the stand or terracing are so important they should stay. The fans certainly take it hard if stars go elsewhere.

The Murdo MacLeod transfer to Germany was a different case from McClair or Johnston. I felt Murdo MacLeod had given the club great service since the time I paid £100,000 for him as a 19-year-old from Dumbarton. In my first five-year spell as manager Murdo also held out on a signing offer and there were even rumours that Rangers were considering bidding for him. But Murdo gave Celtic the best of his career so I was pleased for him that he got such a good deal signing for Borussia Dortmund. Alan McInally, on the other hand, had become a bit off-hand at Parkhead so I wasn't really worried about him going to Aston Villa, although I wished him well.

While all this was going on I had already agreed a deal with Aberdeen for Billy Stark and had talked over terms with the player. But I didn't want to make Billy my first signing the second time around. I felt this would put too much pressure on him and, equally, it wouldn't have been right because the fans could have concluded that Celtic were taking in a lot of money in transfer fees without being prepared to buy in the same range.

Signing Andy Walker first, therefore, became important. He was a young player (born on 6 April 1965) who had been given a good apprenticeship. It was ironic that he was another forward coming to Parkhead from Motherwell. Joe McBride, Dixie Deans and Brian McClair served us very well. Now we were going for a fourth Fir Parker. However, Motherwell did get a good deal for a striker who was really only emerging. We paid £375,000, but I felt it was particularly important to make a signing impact. Since then Andy has gone from strength to strength and proved the wisdom of Celtic's move. I always believed he would become a star player but I didn't realise how quickly he would do so. He really had an astonishingly good first season with Celtic.

It wasn't easy to settle a deal with Motherwell but I could understand their feelings. We had asked in excess of £1 million for McClair and, although we didn't get this amount from Manchester United, we had after all paid Motherwell only £90,000 for him. Since I watched my first senior football at Fir Park I have a great deal of sympathy for them and accepted that, as a big club, we would be pleasantly screwed over the price for Andy. I have no regrets whatever because it was good to have the opportunity to back my judgment.

Chris Morris was a player I had noted with Sheffield Wednesday in my Manchester City days. He had been in and out of the team but he was one I kept watching. He is fast and is at his best going forward. He came into a position occupied in the past by greats like Danny McGrain, but I thought it right to take a gamble on what I had seen. If a manager is not prepared to back his opinion he would be better in some other occupation.

So Chris took part in our pre-season limber-up games in Sweden when we had to go back to basics about team formation. We worked very hard and, bit by bit, things started to go better for us. I look back now and think how quickly Stark, Morris and Walker settled in and the immediate impact they made.

I was, frankly, pleased to be in a job. But even more delighted to be back at Celtic Park which I had thought could never happen. From that point of view it was great but, realistically, I felt we had a battling season ahead of us. I didn't believe then that we could possibly finish top of the table.

The signing of Frank McAvennie on 2 October 1987 was important to our achievements. I phoned John Lyall, the manager of West Ham, for whom I have a lot of respect. He told me he wouldn't even contemplate selling McAvennie but, if he did, he would want £1.5 million. "I couldn't let him go for any less than that," John said to me. "He would be so difficult to replace."

I would have liked Frank to be with Celtic from the start of my second managerial spell at Parkhead but this just wasn't possible. He's the type that I like and needed up front — sharp, quick, aggressive and with a great deal of skill. He also has an outgoing personality which makes him a good man to have around in the dressing-room. When I finally went to clinch a deal I was given the news before leaving for London that Rangers were signing Richard Gough from Spurs for a fee in excess of £1 million. I suppose many thought this put extra pressure on me to get McAvennie, but this wasn't the case. We had set up the arrangement with West Ham very quietly because I wanted pleasantly to surprise our supporters with the help of the media. Rangers' announcement almost took the edge off our good news. It was as if they knew what we were planning and jumped in ahead of us. However, I'm sure it was just a coincidence.

I met Frank at London Airport and had no undue problems

getting him to return to Scotland because he genuinely wanted to play for Celtic. This was a major factor in our favour. Indeed, he had to accept a drop in his basic wage to come to Parkhead. To smooth over this problem I pointed out that the difference in Glasgow lifestyle and cost of living would balance the drop in wages.

At first Frank was a bit sluggish on the park. He had put on weight and had to take off around half a stone. However, returning to Scotland has been great for him as he has all his old ambition back. He has been tremendous because he is such a fine competitor, with the bonus for me that he is a good personality and gets on well with the others. Frank was always a target of mine and I'm glad I persisted.

Talking of transfers, I would like to clear up some myths about Joe Miller, whom we signed in November 1987, from Aberdeen. I first saw him, quite by accident, playing in a boys' tournament at Paisley. I was wandering about looking at different games when I came upon Aberdeen Boys' Club from East Kilbride. Right away, I could see they had two especially talented lads — Joe Miller and Paul Wright. Miller almost took my breath away. I immediately made a thorough investigation about him because I believe that the first sight of a player is often the most decisive.

I found out that Miller came from St Mary's in Abercromby Street, where Brother Walfrid, Celtic's founder, had been a member of the teaching institute of Marist Brothers. It really disappointed me that we had lost this talented youngster because, by then, he had signed forms for Aberdeen. With Bobby Calder and Jimmy Caldwell scouting for the Dons in the West of Scotland they managed to snatch up some very good lads. Subsequently, Joe came to Celtic Boys' Club but he was still committed to Aberdeen.

As I did with Gordon Strachan, I kept young Joe very much in my mind. I watched his development, which was first-class, and this was why Celtic were prepared to go in as positively as we did. Miller has undoubted ability and skill but also has an important rapport with the fans. Very few players have this quality. Jimmy Johnstone had it and so does Charlie Nicholas at Pittodrie. Every club needs at least one player like this. I want Celtic to win every game if it's possible but we must never win in such a fashion that we're unexciting. We want to play the kind of football which will

Mo — A decent enough bloke, but the next thing I heard was that he had joined Nantes.

have the fans saying: "That's brilliant." So we need players with charisma like the Joe Millers and Jimmy Johnstones.

Under Alex Ferguson, Miller had been given the right type of apprenticeship. He worked hard and he was also properly disciplined. In addition to this, I know coach Teddy Scott at Pittodrie and he is a person I respect. Anybody who has been in

90

Teddy's hands would have learned the hard way and with the right basics.

I think Joe's progress at Parkhead will be quite dramatic in the next few years. Equally, Celtic will be good for him because we are a club who will back his flair and individuality. The fact that we also have supporters who will back him to the hilt will help.

When the decision was made to sign Miller I have to admit that the way-going of McClair and Johnston were factors on my side. The directors recognised that we couldn't go on losing stars and not replacing them with at least equal talent. Having embarked on expensive development of the club facilities the board also knew that the team on the pitch was of paramount importance. When we talked about players at a board meeting I was asked: "Who is it you really want?" I said Miller. The directors told me to go ahead.

In fact, we had spoken to Aberdeen months before but they made it clear they would not sell him to Celtic for the obvious reason that they didn't want him appearing against them in the Premier League. Aberdeen were fully aware that the player's contract would be up at the end of the season, but they still didn't want him in a green and white jersey. I understand how they felt.

When I contacted Ian Porterfield again I pointed out that we could sit it out and wait until the player was free to sign for whoever he wanted. Ian knew if this state of play took place Miller would get to know about it. Kenny Dalglish had made a good offer on behalf of Liverpool and Alex Ferguson had signalled that Manchester United were very interested, too. I made it very clear to Ian that I didn't want to be involved in any dirty tricks to get Miller as I had too high a regard for the Aberdeen club. In return Ian gave me a full rundown on the other clubs interested. The Dons asked us for £750,000 but I thought this was too much. Eventually we settled on £650,000 and the whole deal was carried out with the utmost discretion from there on. I have no doubt that Aberdeen changed their minds about selling Joe to us because they felt they might lose out at a tribunal.

Anyway, I was watching Scotland drawing with Bulgaria in Bucharest on TV when I got a phone call at half-time to my home saying Aberdeen had formally accepted our offer. The club wanted only to hold fire until Ian Donald, their vice-chairman who is also a member of the SFA International Committee, returned

91

from Bucharest before making an announcement. The transaction was conducted privately and in a most businesslike manner. I believe that's the way to operate. One of the problems, though, is the fact that the Press watch all of these situations so closely it is difficult to keep a secret.

Freedom of contract has become intriguing as most of us genuinely believe that it's possible to get a bargain by going to a tribunal. My experience in England supports the view that the buying clubs certainly get the benefit in most cases. Tribunals try to rationalise deadlocked deals, but I don't think they really study the market values enough. I thought Manchester United got McClair for a bargain price — £850,000. We were asked by the tribunal chairman to adjourn and try again to fix a price between us. United then increased their offer to £850,000 from £600,000, but this still wasn't acceptable to us. You could have knocked me down with a feather when the tribunal chairman came up with an identical figure.

It is flattering when I hear football people saying I have a Midas touch in my signings. I have certainly been lucky. Take the case of Gordon Strachan. I went to Firhill to see a game in which he was playing while I was still in the Celtic team. Strachan was only a kid in the Dundee side but he looked to me like another Alan Ball. I was amazed. So I kept my eye on him. And when I went to Aberdeen and was looking for players, the memory bank went to work. I felt Strachan had a special appeal about him. He created excitement and, as a defender myself, I've always liked players with this extra ability.

When I watched Strachan I could feel myself rising from my seat with admiration. When I went to Aberdeen at first I either watched him myself or had one of my scouts at his game to confirm earlier opinions. He played Queen of the South in the League Cup when my pal Mike Jackson was the manager at Palmerston. Dundee lost 6-0, but Mike confirmed that Gordon was the one Dens Park player who never lost his appetite for the game despite the scoreline. So I was delighted when I was able to sign him for Aberdeen. I wasn't too surprised when Manchester United later persuaded him to join up at Old Trafford, having assessed his undoubted talents.

Another signing I like to reflect on is Steve Archibald. I know

Gordon Strachan looked to me like another Alan Ball. I was amazed.

Scots fans have never really liked him but I thought he was brilliant and managers such as Alex Ferguson and Terry Venables later confirmed this. I had been thrust into management with Clyde and, no matter how much you may think you are ready for it, none of us really is. I quickly had a look at what I had on the staff. Some of the players had been here, there and everywhere. Others were talented, like Brian Ahern and Joe Ward but, for me, the outstanding one was Archibald. He was quick and aggressive and had good ability on the ball. He was very single-minded but I found him smashing to deal with. He could also be nasty when he wanted on the pitch because he was so competitive. I played him everywhere at Shawfield.

Clyde needed money desperately at the time. Just £20,000 to keep them going. I tried to sell Archibald but couldn't get anyone to take him — including Jock Stein. Davie McParland, then Celtic's assistant manager, said I was too close to the player to which I replied: "I might be close to him but the fella can play."

Bertie Auld phoned me from Firhill about players. I suggested Archibald and asked for £20,000. He came back offering £12,000 with the usual story that the Thistle directors wouldn't allow him any more money. Then, all of a sudden, I was off to Aberdeen and right away made a big mistake. I should have said to Dick Donald, the Aberdeen chairman, the day I joined him to give me the money to buy Archie there and then. I didn't get him until I had been at Pittodrie six months. What an asset he would have been from the start. Aberdeen paid £20,000 and later, of course, sold him to Spurs for £850,000. I've joked with Mr Donald several times since that I should have been given commission but he just laughs it off. I was joking myself, of course.

So back to the Scottish football revolution. We had the tremendous success of Aberdeen under Alex Ferguson which was good for the Dons and Scottish football. This encouraged other teams, including Dundee United and Hearts. However, the fact to be faced is that Celtic and Rangers bring the big crowds. And when we are competing with each other at the top end of the League, pulling in the crowds quite dramatically, then the game in Scotland is in a very buoyant position. There's a spin-off for every team, and especially as clubs now keep home gates. For instance, when we go to a place such as Dunfermline more than half the crowd are Celtic fans. So smaller clubs are getting the revenue from the very healthy position currently existing in Scottish football.

I am not a great admirer of the Premier League but I can't say what would be better. It has improved now that we have reverted to a top league of ten with 36 matches. The 44 games in a league of 12 was far too many. Add cup-ties, European matches and international games and players just couldn't keep up. We have to compete with the big boys down south and to bring in the necessary funds to do this we must have a Premier League. However, I can't think of anything which is ideal, bearing in mind that Scotland is a small country, and there are a limited number of football fans to go round 38 clubs.

People, of course, will always talk about a British League because of the needs of clubs to find finance to buy players, restructure grounds and improve facilities. I have always felt that a British League is inevitable. I don't go along with a British Cup because basically the same Scottish teams would also be involved in European competitions. It would be difficult and complicated. However, the regrettable thing about a British League is that, apart from four or five clubs, Scottish football would merely become a "feeder". In the years when we had what I call "The Good Team" Celtic could only have reached full potential had there been a British League. What is clear, though, is that it will be increasingly difficult to compete against the giants of the game in financial terms in our present domestic set-up.

I say again that I'm very, very proud of my country but my ambitions for Celtic are not merely for the club to be a big fish in the small pond of Scottish football. This is a personal opinion, of course, but I want Celtic, once again, to be a big name in Europe. It is not necessary to have a British set-up to achieve this, which is a good point to emerge from the big spending by a few clubs on our side of the border. The financial enterprise which triggered a football boom in Scotland may be the thing to block a British League. Time will tell.

Scottish football has had a shot in the arm. I would point to the fact that the Celtic board of directors — Jack McGinn (chairman), Kevin Kelly, Jim Farrell, Tom Grant and Chris White — embarked on reconstruction of the stadium in a most ambitious way. It was not a venture which the directors rushed. Our chairman wanted to carry out this work for several years before it was actually begun. It was important for Celtic to show our supporters in a tangible way that the club is prepared at all times to stand up and be counted.

Chapter Seven

Moving in Management

THE first day of April 1977 was eventful because that's when I was offered the job of part-time manager of Clyde. I accepted right away. Apart from business difficulties, which clearly influenced me, a friend, Hugh Birt, had asked for help with the under-16's at Celtic Boys' Club of which he was chairman. I was pleased to oblige and really enjoyed it. Working with youngsters is very rewarding and, in a different world, I would prefer to deal only with kids, rather than senior players, because they are so keen to listen and to learn. They're fun to work with and are very appreciative. It makes you realise that the world isn't as bad as it is often painted.

All of a sudden I had a new zest. In the year I was out of the game I enjoyed being on the other side. Spectating was great and I loved following Celtic. I fancied appearing on TV and talking on radio about matches but, much more, I relished being just an ordinary man in the stand. Celtic Boys' Club gave me an added interest.

Unexpectedly, Willie Dunn phoned to ask if I would be interested in managing Clyde. After I had accepted, lots of my friends asked what I was doing at Shawfield. Well, I have always liked the Dunn family and I had a little bit of a shine for Clyde. They had a good board with a wealth of experience in football, which was good for me. This was my first time going to directors' meetings and seeing how another side of the game was conducted.

Clyde were on their uppers, but I quickly struck up a good relationship with the players, which was important. I remember we had to play Celtic in the Glasgow Cup semi-final at Shawfield which had the bonus of bringing in much-needed cash for the club. I asked Bobby Waddell, who was the assistant manager, what we did for a "change" strip, as the white in both club strips clashed. He said we didn't have one. That was on the Thursday night.

Luckily, I had contacts with Umbro, the sports goods company, from my Celtic days. I phoned Jimmy Terris in Manchester and asked him if he could let me have a set of strips. "When do you need them?" he asked. When I said it was Saturday he pointed out that it didn't leave much time. Clyde colours were white, red and black so he had to use existing stock. Our colour requirements were similar to Manchester City so he sent me a set of their change jerseys by Red Star express parcel service.

Liz and I went to the Central Station in Glasgow on Saturday morning and picked up the parcel. Having watched Neilly Mochan at work for years I immediately checked to make sure all the jerseys were there. Calamity! They were all in the parcel but the number eight was missing. So I had to dash to Lumley's sports shop to buy a figure 8 and — dare I say it! — Liz sewed it on with a slight squint. She wanted to do it over again, but there wasn't time. The man who wore the jersey was Steve Archibald — but he was unaware of the little drama behind the scenes. We lost the game 4-2 but did well until Kenny Dalglish scored after a bit of magic and destroyed the whole thing for us. I often think how unprofessional Clyde would have looked with ten numbered players and one anonymous, particularly as Archibald was the player involved.

I had already released a few players and was looking about for others in the new season when Jock Stein phoned to ask if I would be interested in going to Aberdeen as manager. I said yes. As I put the phone down I said to Liz: "Do you fancy going to Aberdeen?" Since I had rented a house in Troon for the summer holidays she asked why we were switching from the Clyde coast. I had to explain that I was about to be offered the Pittodrie job. At the time, we had a beautiful house in Newton Mearns with splendid neighbours, so a move meant a big upheaval. But, typical of Liz, she said she would go wherever I wanted.

Dick Donald contacted me quickly and we met at the Wheel Inn at Scone in Perthshire. I had spoken to Mr Donald when I played at Aberdeen with Celtic, but it was the first time I had really chatted to him. I was very impressed. Everything was quickly sorted out.

7 October 1978 and Alex Ferguson and I shake hands at Pittodrie. The Dons had just beaten us 4-1. Incidentally, three days before this Jock Stein was appointed Scotland manager after 45 days at Leeds.

Mr Donald said, however, that he had to release the news that night. I had to speak to Clyde first but I couldn't raise any of the board. I would have been embarrassed if they had heard from anybody except me. By good luck I got to John McBeth, a good friend of mine and also a Clyde director, who said not to worry that I had made the right decision. I had stopped at every call-box from Scone to Bridge of Allan before I made contact.

As I hit Glasgow my appointment was announced on the radio. Coming towards Barrowfield, Celtic's training ground, I knew the under-16's, with whom I had been involved, were training so they were really the first to be told by me what was happening. Apart, of course, from the Clyde directors whom I was sorry to leave after only a few months.

At home, I sat down to discuss everything with Liz. As an afterthought she asked what I was to be paid. Suddenly, I realised I hadn't even asked about this in my discussions. However, with Dick Donald it didn't matter. Liz and I simply had a good laugh about it. When I went to Pittodrie to meet the staff and the Press I had to point out, as diplomatically as I could, to Dick Donald that we hadn't talked about salary and a contract. I needn't have worried. He said simply: "You can have what you want . . . three years or five. You tell me." There was no haggling and this included the money aspect. He is a superb man. We struck up an instant relationship which to this day I still enjoy.

I loved Aberdeen. It was my first time away from the West of Scotland and every day was like a holiday. It was my good luck to follow Ally MacLeod. Because of Scotland's World Cup failure in 1978 he seems to have been written off as a manager. Some even regard him as a joke. Far from it. Even as a young, inexperienced manager I could see a lot of the positive things Ally had done at Pittodrie. I realised right away that previous managers — Eddie Turnbull, Jimmy Bonthrone and Ally — had looked after the club very well. Plus the fact that at director level it had been very well run. There were only three directors — Mr Donald, Charlie Forbes and Chris Anderson. Although the personnel have changed, the Pittodrie board is still only three in number with Mr Donald continuing as the boss.

Some of Ally's ideas didn't suit me, of course, as we are entirely different types of people. There were schemes which would have

100

worked for him but not for me. Nevertheless, at Pittodrie there was a very solid base to work on. There were a lot of very good young professionals — lads like Willie Miller, John McMaster, Stewart Kennedy, Ian Fleming and Joe Harper. Joe was controversial but I liked him. He was a bit of a character who needed firm handling, mind you. He had great ability on the pitch and related very well to the fans. Drew Jarvie was one of the more experienced players there and he was good to have around.

The first thing I did at Pittodrie was transfer Arthur Graham to Leeds United. The move had been tied up before I was appointed. It was disappointing because I always fancied Arthur as a player. But he had been told that if the right offer came in he would be allowed to go. So that was it.

In fact, the first player I met at Pittodrie was McMaster. I was introduced to the ground staff and, working with them, was this youngster with blond hair who turned out to be McMaster. What a player he was. I put number 11 on him and the locals couldn't understand it as he clearly wasn't a winger like Graham. They expected John to do the same thing whereas he was a creative midfielder. The crowd gave him terrible stick. In the next game I gave him the number four jersey but fielded him in the same position. He was outstanding and I was applauded for my "vision" in converting John from a winger to such a fine midfielder. In fact, all I had done was change his number! The lesson was that fans relate certain jobs to the number on a player's jersey.

Years after I left Pittodrie John went to Cappielow, but this was also long after a serious knee injury when he clashed with Ray Kennedy, of Liverpool, in a European Cup-tie. Major surgery followed to rejoin the ligaments. I feel that this accident robbed Scotland of a really creative left-sided midfielder. I thought he was magnificent.

In that season, 1977-78, Willie Miller was still a young man. But what a great competitor and determined tackler he was even then. He was as hard as nails. Miller had very few ordinary performances and the great thing about him is that he doesn't miss many games. He is a real solid person and, not surprisingly, has been a cornerstone for the club. Most of Aberdeen's success, indeed, has stemmed from the fact that Willie and Alex McLeish are so good at the heart of the defence.

When I went to Aberdeen McLeish was only a youngster. People used to laugh at Ally MacLeod's extravagant forecasts, but he said that Big Alex would play for Scotland. He wasn't ready for the first team when I was at Pittodrie but he has since fully justified Ally's opinion. Willie Garner, in fact, was the centre-half, with Miller beside him.

In my first season with the Dons we finished as runners-up to Rangers in the League and the Scottish Cup. Yet we were unbeaten in our opening 11 games and our first defeat was at home to RWD Molenbeck, who beat us 2-1 in the first round of the UEFA Cup after drawing 0-0 in the first leg away from home. In the third round of the League Cup we were hammered 6-1 by Rangers at Ibrox but turned the tables 3-1 in the second leg with Drew Jarvie getting a couple of goals.

My debut as manager in the Premier League was a game against Rangers and we beat them 3-1 at Pittodrie. It was a good start. Later in the season they won 3-1 at Ibrox, then we turned the tables 4-0 at Pittodrie and in the final fixture between us the Dons won 3-0 in Glasgow. So going into the Cup final on 6 May 1978, I felt Aberdeen had a very good chance.

We lost 2-1 in front of 61,563 at Hampden and there is no doubt the Dons froze on the big occasion. At half-time I tried to talk and reason with them. This may have been a mistake. Maybe I was too soft. Had I blistered the players, made them determined to show me up for my opinions, the result could have been different. Perhaps I should also have been trying to hustle the team by telling them about the thousands who had travelled from the Granite City to see them playing so badly. I opted for the encouraging line. We'll never know, of course, what might have happened had I just let rip.

Yet the Dons were a side full of fighting characters such as Stewart Kennedy, Ian Fleming, Willie Miller and goalie Bobby Clark. But Alex MacDonald, now the successful manager of Hearts, tore the heart out of Aberdeen with the kind of opening goal that only a player with exceptional reflexes can score. Robert Russell, who had a great game for Rangers, sent the ball floating goalwards and MacDonald, seeing his chance, sprinted forward to head it past Clark.

Early in the second half Tommy McLean, better known as the

Feeling good after one of our most satisfying wins over Rangers. The date was 21 May 1978 and the 4-2 victory meant a championship victory by three points from the Ibrox club.

Motherwell manager nowadays, left-footed the ball across goal and Derek Johnstone headed it fiercely for Rangers' second. Stevie Ritchie got Aberdeen's goal five minutes from the end when it was really too late to mean anything. Ritchie thrust out his foot at a short pass from McMaster near the goal. He mishit the ball but sent it spinning into the air over the head of Peter McCloy. It dipped, hit the crossbar and bounced down to slip over the line.

The teams that day were: *Rangers*: McCloy, Jardine, Jackson, Forsyth, Greig, Russell, MacDonald, McLean, Johnstone, Smith, Cooper. Subs: Watson (77 mins), Robertson. *Aberdeen*: Clark, Kennedy, Garner, Miller, Ritchie, Sullivan, McMaster, Jarvie, Fleming, Harper, Davidson. Subs: Scanlon (56 mins), McClelland.

One surprising "inheritance" from Ally MacLeod at Pittodrie was a situation where the club had four goalkeepers: Bobby Clark, Ally McLean, John Garner and Jim Leighton. It was impossible to handle as we had only two teams. So I put Leighton out to the Highland League club Deveronvale, who weren't good at the time. Ken Tedcastle, an Englishman by the way, was in charge. Sending players to the Highland clubs is a good facility for the Dons. Willie Miller is another who went there to gain experience. Teddy Scott made the Leighton arrangement.

In Jim's first game Deveronvale were beaten by a big score and I wondered if I was giving him the right preparation. However, Jim settled in so well — and typical of the type of person he is — that Deveronvale's results began to change dramatically. In fact, at the end of the season they won one of the Cup competitions. At Pittodrie, we began to be almost as interested in Deveronvale's results as we were in our own. I feel that this spell helped Jim to forge himself into the great 'keeper he became with Aberdeen and Scotland and now, of course, Manchester United.

Jim was never in the first team during my Aberdeen stint, but Alex McLeish made his debut against Dundee United. Willie Garner and Bobby Glennie were left out after a game against Clydebank at Kilbowie at New Year which we won 1-0. Quite simply, they hadn't been as strict with themselves as I asked them to be. The Dundee United game followed quickly on the Monday so I took a chance and pulled in Alex and Doug Rougvie. We won 1-0 again with a goal by Ian Fleming after Rougvie had made a run down the right with only five minutes to go. I thought from then on it was certain that McLeish was going to be a star player — as predicted by Ally.

We enjoyed life in Aberdeen. It was a lovely experience for my family, even if it was only for a year. The oil boom was just taking off then, but I don't think this had anything to do with the enjoyment the place and the people gave us. So when the call came from Celtic there was a good deal of reluctance in my family to move back to Glasgow. Liz was particularly keen on the way of life in Aberdeen and at Stonehaven where we actually had our home. From the point of view of my development as a manager, it might have been better to have stayed longer at Pittodrie.

It was probably unfair of Big Jock to come to me at that particular time. After all, I had offered my services to him at Parkhead, but he had given no indication that he, or the club, were interested. My time at Aberdeen was successful but all of a sudden

MOVING IN MANAGEMENT

I was on my way back to Celtic. I remember being in the North British Hotel in Glasgow with Aberdeen director Chris Anderson, for whom I had a great respect, and I really felt guilty that I couldn't tell him about an approach made to me at the writers' dinner at the Albany Hotel which we had both attended. John Colrain and Mike Jackson also came to see me, but I couldn't say a word to anyone.

It would, however, have been a big gamble if I had turned Celtic down. The opportunity might never have come again. For me that would have been terrible because I can say unreservedly that Celtic have always been the club for me. I was only 38 when I returned to Parkhead and even then I felt I was still fit enough to have played.

My heart certainly ruled my decision. At Aberdeen I was allowed to do the things I thought were right. I also had good players whom I knew would develop. It is to Alex Ferguson's credit that he continued the work so well, although at first he tried to convert them to the style he had operated at St Mirren. He soon realised this wasn't the right way and switched tactics.

With my feelings and my attitude to Celtic I just couldn't say "no". Perhaps I should have looked at the position on a long-term basis, but opportunities in life must be grabbed.

I never did sign a contract with Aberdeen although, after a couple of bad results around October, I was assured by Mr Donald there was no problem. I never went back to him on the subject. However, I must say that a manager's confidence can be shaken by poor results. I'm not sure how I would have handled it if Mr Donald had asked me to think again about going to Celtic. But I realised this wasn't his style. Stuart Spence, his son-in-law, told me he had suggested to Mr Donald that he should approach me to stay, but the chairman said he didn't want to do anything which would prevent me doing something I might regret later.

When I returned to Celtic Park in May 1978, I couldn't believe how low the standard had sunk. I had teamed with players of quality, class and character, but I was deeply disappointed looking at the side which it was now my job to improve. They had just had their poorest season for 13 years and I wasn't surprised. They had finished only fifth in the League, which is not Celtic form. However, they did suffer three big set-backs. Kenny Dalglish went to Liverpool for £440,000 — the bargain of the decade — Pat

Stanton received an injury in the opening League match which forced him to retire, and Danny McGrain missed all but the first seven games. This cost him a place in the ill-fated World Cup team in Argentina.

Parkhead was dead.

I had arranged to take Jimmy Lumsden, of Clydebank, to Pittodrie to help Teddy Scott. But I needed him with Celtic much more, basically to play in the reserves and help bring youngsters along. He ended up playing in the first team. I talked to the board and they said there would be around £200,000 available for transfers, but this wouldn't have bought anything like what was needed. I paid £120,000 for Davie Provan right away and followed up with another £100,000 for Murdo MacLeod, but they were only youngsters.

I badgered and hammered the players right through the season and we really dragged ourselves to the top of the Premier League after recording only seven wins in our first 18 matches. Bobby Lennox rejoined the club from America and Vic Davidson came back from Blackpool. Danny McGrain was able to return to first-team action in the latter part of the season.

Our end-of-the-season match with Rangers was like a fiction writer's dream. To win the League Rangers needed one point when we met at Celtic Park in front of 52,000. Celtic needed two. Alex MacDonald scored in nine minutes and, as if this wasn't bad enough, Johnny Doyle was ordered off ten minutes after half-time. He became involved with MacDonald and I remember telling poor "Doylie" that if Celtic lost he would be in very serious trouble. I was furious because it had been stupid to be sent off, especially when we were in such a desperate position.

The team showed unbelievable character, though. Roy Aitken pulled the score back to 1-1. I subbed Bobby Lennox for Mike Conroy and Rangers replied by bringing on Alex Miller for Tommy McLean. Then George McCluskey hammered in a second goal after an Aitken drive had been blocked. 2-1 and I could hardly believe it. Robert Russell quickly levelled, though. We had to wait until five minutes from the end before Colin Jackson headed the ball past his own 'keeper, Peter McCloy, after a McCluskey effort had been pushed out. Then, with a minute to go Murdo MacLeod got the ball. On the bench we were shouting to him to kick it

If you think I'm consoling Jim McLean, I'm not. We had just lost 3-0. But we still won the title with 40 points — 15 ahead of United.

anywhere for safety. Murdo couldn't hear us in the din, of course, but he did play safe. He hit the ball right into the roof of the net.

In the foyer afterwards Jimmy Johnstone, Bobby Murdoch, Mike Jackson, Paul Wilson, Pat McCluskey, Benny Rooney and a lot of other old Celts were dancing around in amazement. It was as though they had been playing. We won that extraordinary game with sheer character and drive. It wasn't class that did it, but it was tremendous all the same. I think the teams are worth putting down for posterity: *Celtic*: Latchford, McGrain, Lynch, Aitken, McAdam, Edvaldsson, Provan, Conroy (Lennox), McCluskey, MacLeod, Doyle. *Rangers*: McCloy, Jardine, Dawson, Johnstone, Jackson, MacDonald, McLean (Miller), Russell, Parlane, Smith, Cooper.

Soon after this the team went on a sunshine holiday to Majorca. Neilly Mochan said to me: "Only one thing worries me. Maybe you've done too much too quickly. You weren't entitled to win the League."

In the next season, 1970-80, we threw the championship away but won the Scottish Cup. I tried to extend and strengthen our first team squad and one signing was Dom Sullivan for £80,000 from Aberdeen. I was searching for class because, as I've already said, we were winning by sheer determination and aggression. Sullivan came into the team against Rangers at Parkhead the day after he joined us. Roddie MacDonald headed the only goal 14 minutes from the end and Sullivan added some silky touches to our play.

In March, we bought Frank McGarvey from Liverpool for a then record £250,000 fee and just beat the signing deadline. There had been a tremendous turnover of players at reserve level as well as the first team.

Our start that season was not the most auspicious as we could only beat Morton 3-2, with Andy Ritchie scoring both goals for the Cappielow club, the second four minutes from the end. A crowd of 26,000 indicated that the fans were in a state of expectancy. We then went to Ibrox and drew 2-2, which was a notable result because we were down 2-0 and hit back with goals by Alan Sneddon and Tom McAdam in the last six minutes. Roy Aitken had been sent off in 36 minutes, so again the team showed they had the right kind of ambition.

A 5-0 win against Kilmarnock, with George McCluskey scoring

a hat-trick, set us up for a good run from late August. We won 3-1 at Easter Road and then 2-1 at Pittodrie, and again the victory against the Dons had to be achieved with ten men as Tommy Burns was red-carded 11 minutes from half-time. Roy Aitken and Johnny Doyle got our goals.

The most significant games we had to play were against Real Madrid in the quarter-final of the European Cup. We had knocked out Partizan Tirana, of Albania, and the Irish club Dundalk. Indeed, things were going marvellously well at this stage. In front of 67,000 at Parkhead we beat the great Real 2-0 and then went to Bernabeu Stadium in Madrid. A crowd 110,000 were there to watch. We played well. George McCluskey made a couple of great chances early on, and one in particular could have killed the game stone dead.

I remember talking to Bob Paisley, of Liverpool, before going to Madrid and he made the point that we would have difficulty with the Hungarian referee Koroli Palotai, especially as the game was in Spain. He was right. Mr Palotai was as disappointing as the result and the two factors were not totally unconnected. Among other things, Benito clearly handled in the penalty box, but this was ignored. In the first half we had Real struggling and, apart from the fact that we hadn't managed to score, everything seemed to be going well until the last few seconds when Santillana scored for the Spaniards after the referee had given a free-kick against Peter Latchford for time-wasting.

In the dressing-room I could see from the expressions of our players how disappointed they were to have lost a goal. So I had to work on building up their confidence by stressing how well they had done. However, in the second half Stielike and Juantino scored for Real, so our European dream was over for another season.

Afterwards we never recovered our League form and the season died a death for us, despite winning the Scottish Cup with a dramatic extra-time goal by George McCluskey. Frankly, I hadn't realised the impact losing to Real would have on the side.

We had lost 2-1 at Parkhead against Aberdeen and this was the most significant result. Bobby Lennox took a penalty which Bobby Clark saved easily. Early in the second half Tom McAdam had to go off with concussion. This meant Roy Aitken had to move into the defence and his power was missed in midfield. Aberdeen pipped us for the title by a single point, so that penalty failure could well have cost us the championship. However, our most disappointing result was losing 5-1 at Dens Park.

Winning the Cup was some consolation — and especially as it was against Rangers. Johannes Edvaldsson had gone earlier in the season and Roddie MacDonald and Tom McAdam were both ineligible. We were left without a recognised centre-half. Jim Casey was to play in the position but injured himself in training. So I made Mike Conroy the centre-half and, despite the doubters, Conroy emerged as the unlikely superstar of the match.

McCluskey's goal certainly brought joy to the Celtic fans in the crowd of 70,303. Danny McGrain hit the ball first time for goal. Peter McCloy probably had it covered, but George stuck out his left foot to send it into the far corner. The teams on that memorable afternoon were: *Celtic*: Latchford, Sneddon, McGrain Aitken, Conroy, MacLeod, Provan, Doyle (Lennox), McCluskey, Burns, McGarvey (Davidson). *Rangers*: McCloy, Jardine, Dawson, Forsyth (Miller), Jackson, Stevens, Cooper, Russell, Johnstone, Smith, J MacDonald (McLean).

Interestingly, in the fourth round we had to replay St Mirren after a 1-1 draw at Parkhead and Tom McAdam was sent off, so we had to win 3-2 in extra-time with ten men. Before the semi-final against Hibs we went to Seamill and I had a real head-to-header with the players. I fell out with Tommy Burns, a player I admire on and off the pitch. He felt I was picking on him, which wasn't true. We won 5-0, coasting to a convincing win and Tommy came on as a sub for Bobby Lennox. My words had paid off.

I enjoyed working with these players. It's been said that I was too hard on them. If I was it was the mistake of a young manager. I was still in my late thirties but, at the time, I felt I had to be tough. Apart from Bobby Lennox and Danny McGrain we had a very young side.

So we salvaged something from the season, but perhaps we should have anticipated failure in the League. I recalled what Neilly had said in Majorca. The signing of McGarvey came too late to give him time to settle in properly. Charlie Nicholas was the most talented star with whom I've worked, but no player has given me more enjoyment than McGarvey. He is one of these delightful characters who brings fun to the dressing-room. I'm not convinced that Frank knew what he was doing himself all the time, but he was a guy I liked having around. He was always active and was a hard worker on the pitch.

Our 1980-81 season started out with all sorts of promise. And, of course, we were to win back the championship. We beat Morton and Kilmarnock, but then lost 2-1 to Rangers when Alex Miller scored in the last minute with an incredible shot in a game which we should have had well and truly tied up. The players didn't let this upset them and they played methodically towards the title.

Aberdeen, being champions, took the early ascendancy, which was a reversal of the previous season. However, we had some very good results and in April had to go to Ibrox needing at least a point to sew up the championship. Charlie Nicholas won the game with a beautiful solo run in which he took on the defence and then sent his shot raging past Jim Stewart in Rangers' goal.

We won the League by seven points and, when I look back on my first five-year stint with Celtic, we finished twice behind Aberdeen and Dundee United and, in each of the two seasons, it was because of our own mistakes. Consider the fact that the Dons topped the table with 48 points to our 47 but the following year we had 56 and the Dons 49.

The significant thing about this season was the advent of Nicholas. He was the most prominent of several youngsters whom we tried. Charlie came on in that game at Ibrox as a substitute, replacing McGarvey, and he made a terrific impact apart from his spectacular goal. He gave us confirmation that what we were doing at grassroots level was right and would be important to the club. Nicholas was my first real chance to bring in an especially talented youngster. I could be accused of being that little bit slow in giving him his chance, but the truth is I recognised an outstanding talent and worried about the best time to introduce him.

I'll let you into a secret. In my Aberdeen days I tried to sign Charlie, who was then still unattached. I wanted him on a schoolboy form. He was with Celtic Boys' Club, but was not committed to Celtic. But as soon as I made the move Celtic grabbed his signature. I think it was my bid which alerted Celtic to

Charlie, Charlie . . . with Roy Aitken.

sign him, because I'm not sure they realised the talent they had right in front of them.

Charlie always appealed to me. He delights crowds as well as

112

getting goals. He is one of the élite who has supporters in a nearly constant state of excitement. As a young lad he was cocky, cheerful and confident. The only thing I worried about was his eccentric dress style. Maybe it was the first indication that I was getting that wee bit older.

There were all kinds of stories about me fining Charlie. So I might as well admit his habit of not wearing socks upset me. I confess I made him stump up for this. The style had just come in, but I thought it was basically unhygienic. In establishing discipline I've never been too rigid. The system must be designed to give the players a bit of fun as well as punishing them. Charlie always understood this and took it the right way. I told Charlie that if I caught him without socks it would cost him. He took the hint and started wearing them again. However, I found out he was driving to the park without socks and putting them on in his car before coming to the dressing-room. I waited my opportunity. Seeing him leaving the ground I gave him just enough time to take his socks off in his car and then sent someone to ask him to come back to see me urgently. And, yes, he was sockless, so he had to pay up! But he knew it was also part of the dressing-room jollity.

I'm convinced that Charlie deliberately provoked me. One day he wore a poncho which looked like a hand-me-down from Clint Eastwood. I told Charlie, looking as stern as I could, that he had gone too far and that I wouldn't accept players dressing like this. Charlie's gear made him look as though he was on holiday 52 weeks of the year. But if he was required to appear at supporters' functions he was immaculate — and this included wearing a collar and tie.

In case you think I'm obsessed about dress, I have a belief that being smart in appearance at the right times is important. It puts you at a psychological advantage. This applies even to the outfits players wear for matches.

Charlie always takes a delight in going to meet fans and he was able to identify with them easily. In some ways he was like a character from the pages of *Roy of the Rovers*. He exploded on the scene in my third season as Celtic manager and was exactly what I wanted in a star — exciting, brimming over with personality, talent, the lot. Unquestionably, he is the most skilled youngster with whom I have worked. Maybe it's because I'm a defender that I

so admire a front player with genuine flair. Celtic school lads
believe that winning is important, but doing it with panache is so
much more desirable.

The thing that I don't think fans appreciate is that Charlie is a
very hard worker. He leads the line well and is still doing so at
Pittodrie. He is an instinctive player who doesn't need to look
round to see where the ball was. He knows. He also scores good
goals — not just blasting the ball in, but seeing a space and guiding
it past the goalie. He was transferred to Arsenal on 22 June 1983,
making the announcement while touring with Scotland in Canada.
Six days later Dom Sullivan was given a free and another two days
passed before I was on the move myself.

Charlie's ability had been noticed. And the fact that he was
coming to the end of his contract at Parkhead inspired interest
from Liverpool, Manchester United and Arsenal. The calibre of
the clubs who wanted to buy him merely confirmed my view about
his skills. Celtic tried hard to get Charlie to stay at Parkhead. But
our offer, good at that time for us, palled in comparison to what the
English teams were prepared to pay. Reports at the time claimed
that Charlie was being guaranteed £400,000 basic pay over four
years which was a fortune in our language. Bonuses could take this
figure to £500,000, whereas we were talking around £40,000 a year
basic plus perks.

The disappointing aspect for me was that I genuinely didn't
think Charlie was ready to move. I gave him advice as his manager
and also as a friend. I warned him he might not like what I said, but
he didn't have to accept it. Obviously, he had great talent and was
entitled to earn big money. However, I didn't feel he had
accomplished enough at Parkhead and I wanted him to give the
punters that little bit extra.

Charlie countered reasonably that he could get huge sums of
money immediately. I argued that nobody would be able to stop him
being a big earner whether he went now or in a year or two. I
thought he should be more mature and experienced before he went
south.

Charlie broke a leg in January 1982, and this may have made him
wary about the future. I criticised myself for playing him in the
reserves at Cappielow. He had gone off form a little and I fielded
him in tricky conditions to try to keep his form up. He broke his leg

in an accidental clash with Joe McLaughlin. That was when I saw another side of Charlie. He accepted his misfortune cheerfully and worked very hard, with the help of our physio Brian Scott, to be fit again. He built up his body and made himself much stronger.

Overall, Charlie made an extraordinary impression on the football scene in three short years which included the time he was off recovering from the leg-break. You will now ask why he didn't really hit the heights with Arsenal. I think he went there with such a fanfare that even a vastly more experienced player with a cosmopolitan background would have found it difficult to excel. He was truly the glamour boy who captured the imagination of British football. Initially, that made it difficult for him. Equally, Arsenal weren't the most renowned club for attractive football and I think he found it difficult to adapt to their style. He also went with a reputation for scoring great goals like the one for Scotland in their 2-2 draw with Switzerland on his international debut.

He went to London for a £625,000 fee, but was still regarded as a £1 million player. He had also turned down Liverpool and Manchester United and not too many stars get the chance to do that. He went to Arsenal by choice, having left Celtic where the fans adored him. He took himself into a difficult situation, which was perhaps not improved by the fact that he had an agent who involved him in things he would have been better keeping at arm's length.

He was wrongly marketed. A playboy image was not the one for Charlie. He went to Arsenal, I believe, because his agent steered him to London. He was not sure about trying to fill Kenny Dalglish's boots at Liverpool — and I don't blame him for that — and Manchester United had talked about enlarging their pool whereas Charlie wanted to be in a first team.

Why did Charlie not return to Parkhead when it became clear he was to leave Arsenal? I didn't feel he had developed in England as he should have. It is not possible to be specific about the reason. Was it the style of Arsenal? The good life in the bright lights of London overtaking him? Or, perhaps, was he simply not the hungry youngster who had left Scotland so starry-eyed? I don't think he was as good a player at the end of his Arsenal period as he was when he left Celtic. And his appetite for the game didn't seem as keen.

However, having lost McClair and Johnston, I realised that we needed ability and personality. I was prepared to gamble that coming back to Parkhead would provide Charlie with the right platform to rekindle all his old fire and determination. But I had to be sure in my mind that he wanted to return to Celtic. People have said I discussed money with him, but this isn't so. I asked quite simply if he would come back, or if he wanted to stick with it at Arsenal under Scot George Graham. He was perfectly honest and told me he wanted to have another stab at making it at Highbury. I had no intention of going out of my way to persuade him. I didn't want him to play for us for the wrong reasons. His attitude, and not the pot of gold we might have offered him, was the only thing important.

When Charlie finally became available I had distanced myself from the problem to have a better chance to think. By this time the board had authorised me to buy players who genuinely wanted to join our club and one of them, of course, was Frank McAvennie. I took fresh faces in and they haven't let me down.

There is no doubt that, at the start of the 1987-88 season, if Charlie had given me indications he wanted to be with Celtic again, I would have signed him. When he went to Aberdeen I was a bit nervous about what he might do but at the end of the day I had to make judgments and couldn't be influenced because spectators liked the sound of a name. I didn't return to Celtic to have decisions thrust upon me by other people — much as I respect the fans of our club.

Charlie's last game for Celtic was against Finn Harp at Donegal in the Republic of Ireland. As it happened it turned out to be my last, too, before being "exiled" to England for nearly four years. Sadly, he confirmed he was going. So an era ended — and I hope that Charlie has as much success, and provides the same amount of entertainment, for Aberdeen as he did in his days at Parkhead. That way nobody will be disappointed.

We won the championship for a 33rd time in season 1981-82 after leading from start to finish. In our preparation we played in a prestigious tournament in Holland in which we had to oppose Feyenoord, Anderlecht and Dukla Prague. It was apparent before we kicked off that it was supposed to be an Anderlecht-Feyenoord final. The Dutch were disappointed. Although Celtic and Dukla

Poolside with Charlie Nicholas and Mo Johnston.

were there merely to make up the numbers we beat Feyenoord in the first round and Dukla won against Anderlecht. In the final we beat the Czechs convincingly, which led me to think our season would start well and that we would be in good European form because Feyenoord were a very prominent team at that time.

But we found ourselves in a League Cup section against St Mirren, St Johnstone and Hibs and, to my consternation, began disastrously. We lost at home to St Mirren and away to St Johnstone but beat Saints at Paisley 5-1 and licked St Johnstone 4-1 at Parkhead then failed to qualify by a point even though we beat Hibs 4-1 home and away. We scored 18 goals and conceded nine so we really tumbled out because St Mirren beat us 3-1 in the opener.

We redressed the balance by winning our first seven League games, including going to Pittodrie in our second match and winning 3-1 which was important. We then went to Ibrox and won 2-0 with goals by Tom McAdam and Murdo MacLeod. So our fortunes changed dramatically and we ended up winning the flag by two points from Aberdeen. That campaign was terrific for us but another disappointing aspect was being beaten in the fourth round of the Scottish Cup by a John Hewitt goal for Aberdeen.

In the European Cup we beat Juventus with a Murdo MacLeod goal in front of 60,000 at Parkhead. But, in Turin, Virdis and Bettega scored against us in a match in which we could have had a couple of penalties. Danny McGrain had damaged his ankle so it was a big blow to be without him in Italy. David Moyes made his European debut and played very well. Liam Brady gave a positively incredible performance for the Italian club. I had been a long-time admirer of Irishman Brady and wasn't surprised by the quality of his display. But without him that night Celtic could well have been in the second round.

In October of that season the club was shattered by the death, in an accident at home, of Johnny Doyle. It was tragic, and while we mourned for Johnny we also felt deeply for his family.

My fifth season at the Parkhead helm, 1982-83, ended with Celtic pipped by a point by Dundee United who won their first championship. We threw it away by losing to United (3-2) and Aberdeen (1-0) in the space of three days on the critical run-in period in April. In the United game Graeme Sinclair was carried off with concussion and Ralph Milne lobbed a cheeky winner near the end. And it was that man Mark McGhee who got the Aberdeen winner in 34 minutes at Pittodrie.

We did win the League Cup but I was to find out that wasn't enough . . . even though it was after a 2-1 tussle with Rangers at Hampden. Charlie Nicholas and Murdo MacLeod, with a thundering shot after a half-clearance by Dave MacKinnon, scored for us in the first half and Jim Bett got Rangers' goal soon after half-time from a free-kick. The teams on a drab day at Hampden were: *Celtic*: Bonner, McGrain, Sinclair, Aitken, McAdam, MacLeod, Provan, McStay (Reid), McGarvey, Burns, Nicholas. *Rangers*: Stewart, MacKinnon, Redford, McClelland, Paterson, Bett, Cooper, Prytz (Dawson), Johnstone, Russell (MacDonald), Smith.

In the European Cup we eliminated Johan Cruyff's Ajax, who had won the tournament three times, and then took on Real Sociedad. In the first leg in Spain the Basques scored twice in four minutes in the latter part of the game and, at Parkhead, Celtic won 2-1 on the night — Murdo MacLeod got both goals — but committed suicide by gifting the Spanish champions a vital away goal in only 25 minutes.

So my record after five years was three League championships and the Scottish Cup and League Cup once each. Most managers would be very happy with that but I looked for more.

Chapter Eight

South of the Border

MY "exile" to England lasted nearly four years, three with Manchester City followed by eight bewildering months at Aston Villa before being sacked by an autocratic chairman. I returned to Scotland a good deal wiser and believe I am a better manager because of the experience.

I never expected to go south in the first place. But a personality clash between myself and the late Desmond White, the club chairman, mysteriously built up. I am not saying I was right in everything, but I am still baffled and regretful that it reached such an extent that I had to leave. I am discussing this now as a matter of record. It would be dishonest in an autobiography to dodge an issue which was such an important milestone in my career. Happily, the situation has been resolved in the manner I always hoped it would be — by me returning to the club which has been such an important part of my life. The fact that I have been able to do so says much for the magnanimity and mature good sense of the directors.

The story of what turned out to be my departure from Celtic began when I played in the first Glasgow Open Golf Championship at Haggs Castle. I was pleased about how good the tournament was for Glasgow which is my "adopted" city because, of course, I was born in Bellshill. Coming off the course, after partnering Howard Clark, I was asked unexpectedly by a group of reporters about a move to Manchester City. The truth was I had been sounded out quietly but had brushed the question aside without expressing any interest. So I was taken aback that the Press had got wind of a private, and at that stage not too serious approach, although I could see it was to City's advantage to have it in the papers that they were inquiring about me.

Two days later, on a Monday, I attended a meeting in Mr White's office in Bath Street. Most of the directors were also present. I went naïvely, thinking there was no major problem and certainly none which would lead to me leaving Parkhead. I had refused to comment on the City approach to the papers and was, therefore, shocked to see some of the headlines which included this one: "McNeill demands a wage increase." I never demanded anything. What I had done was ask the chairman twice if I could be included in a pensions scheme. I never received an answer.

Quite a lot of my private business became public. The fact that I was being paid £20,000 a year and that I owed the club £11,000, part of an interest-free loan, was freely discussed in the media. The latter fact emerged in an official statement from Celtic. Some writers even pointed out that I was well down the salary scale in the Premier League. The Press were saying this, mark you, not me.

At the meeting it was quickly clear that my future was secondary. The room was littered with Sunday papers and I was accused of making statements which I was required to deny. Since I had done no such thing I pointed out that I couldn't be responsible for the work of newspaper sub-editors. I did want my conditions improved so that I was at least in a comparable position to other leading Premier League managers. I certainly was not looking for fortunes and had not "demanded" anything.

The media claimed that John Greig, Jim McLean, Alex Ferguson and Ricky McFarlane at St Mirren were better off. I have to be honest and say it got my back up that the meeting with the board had turned so badly against me that all they wanted were apologies for what had been reported. I felt I was being manoeuvred into a position where the chairman wanted me to walk out. I was shattered when I left the meeting.

Pride has always been my spur. I don't like letting anybody down and I don't fancy being let down myself. I was asked to eat humble pie and I couldn't see that I had done anything, or said anything, to warrant this. I was never given the opportunity to spell out what I thought was reasonable by way of a better salary scale. It seemed to me that Mr White wanted a parting of the ways. His mind was made up.

Part of the background to all this was that, at a previous meeting, Mr White said he wanted me to sack John Clark as assistant manager and appoint Frank Connor who later got the job under Davie Hay, only to be removed himself. I had nothing against Frank and, having worked with him previously, knew his capabilities and his love of Celtic. I do, however, believe that a manager should be the judge of his working assistant. I asked for time to think, but my immediate reaction was to say no. I had a week's holiday in the west coast of Scotland which gave me the chance to ponder the whole scenario quietly. I decided that it was important for me to retain the right to appoint an assistant. So I declined to do what I had been asked. I warned John what had been going on and he was naturally very upset.

I wasn't even told the transfer fee paid by Arsenal for Charlie Nicholas. The chairman asked me to tell the Press that Celtic and Arsenal had "satisfactorily" agreed on a transfer fee, but he would not reveal the amount — even to me, his manager. I disagreed with the way the Nicholas transfer was handled anyway. We should have taken Arsenal to a tribunal. However, it seemed that my integrity was being questioned since I wasn't trusted with the information about the fee.

My position as manager was being usurped and this was underlined when I tried to sign Joe McLaughlin from Morton. Benny Rooney and Mike Jackson talked about £250,000 which I wouldn't look at. It was simply too much, but Morton needed cash and they were trying to get the best deal. Some time later Benny phoned to say I could have the player for £85,000. This time I thought the price was right. With Morton's blessing I established from Joe that he wanted to join Celtic rather than Chelsea, who were also in the bidding. I phoned Mr White, who said, reasonably, that he had to consult the other directors. Eventually, Mr White came back with the news that the board had turned down the idea of buying McLaughlin. I then spoke again to the player and wished him every good luck with Chelsea, for whom he has since been a very good player indeed.

So I was either being squeezed out or stripped of authority which would be unacceptable to any worthwhile manager. Mr White's parting shot after the meeting in his office was: "You can have further discussions with whichever club you wish." So my days with

A formidable trio: me, Jock Stein and John Clark.

Celtic were officially numbered.

Soon afterwards I met Peter Swales, the Manchester City chairman, in Carlisle. But, even then, I asked for time to have another chat with Celtic. He gave me 24 hours, but was on the telephone next morning trying to get a quick decision. I contacted Mr White, told him the exact position and asked if he had altered his thoughts. He came back offering to up my salary to £25,000, but insisting that Frank Connor became assistant manager and that I retracted statements in the papers. Within a few minutes I told Mr Swales that he had a new City manager.

My troubles may well have stemmed from an incident between me and a reporter while we were on the way to a European game in Hungary. More about this later. I did offer my resignation twice at the time but this was not taken up.

I tried to clear the air with Mr White, making the point that our troubles did not seem to be related to negotiations about either money or a contract. Mr White finally said that he felt I "overplayed" my authority at times.

The relationship between a manager and the chairman is very important, and perhaps I should have tried even harder to ensure it worked at Parkhead. However, it was difficult to team up with Mr White. I asked him more than once if we could meet on a regular basis to talk about the running of the club, and preferably away from Celtic Park, but this never happened. There should be a better understanding between chairman and manager.

I admit I wasn't properly prepared for the Celtic job. It would have been better if I had been longer at Pittodrie. I tended to ride roughshod over things, and maybe even people. More diplomacy was required from me. With hindsight I can understand why Mr White was sometimes aggrieved. I even stormed out of a board meeting because the discussion became too explosive.

To be truthful, I wasn't the easiest individual to get on with, but nobody could ever doubt that I wanted the best for Celtic. The players thought I was hard on them and, perhaps, in some ways I was. My only reason was that I badly wanted Celtic to be successful and I was prepared to sacrifice popularity to help obtain this. I still believe in discipline, but I've learned from past events. Maybe I was too impatient. And, remember, when we lost to Aberdeen and Dundee United in the championship in my first five years it was to vastly improved teams — one of whom later won the Cup Winners' Cup and the other reaching the UEFA Cup final. It was a time when the north-east was trying very hard to end the Old Firm domination.

The Celtic board knew me well enough, however. I had, after all, been a player at Parkhead for 18 years. I wasn't a new boy by any means. Throughout my career I've been fiery, but I've always aimed at being good for Celtic.

At Aberdeen, I had a great understanding with chairman Dick Donald and director Chris Anderson. Both of them helped me a lot. This is the kind of relationship a manager needs. Without it the job can be very lonely indeed. I'm delighted to say I'm now given every help by our directors and chairman Jack McGinn with whom my relations are excellent.

As I left for the south I felt the playing side at Parkhead was coming together and Brian McClair had been bought to demonstrate that there was life after Charlie Nicholas. However I was on my way, in a shattered state, to Maine Road. My world had been turned upside down. It happened so quickly that a pal, planning to put a brick barbecue in the garden of the house I had owned for all of six weeks, couldn't get it done before I departed. He had planned it as a house-warming gift!

In my early days in Manchester — in June 1983 — I was unbelievably lonely. Looking at the list of supporters' clubs I invariably forgot myself and referred to them as Celtic fans instead of City. It was all part of me being homesick.

I was so fed up when the pre-season training kicked off, and I was still living in a hotel, that I packed everything and drove to Glasgow. I told Liz I wasn't going back, that I had taken enough. I had been in Manchester only a few weeks and was thoroughly homesick. Liz, however, pointed out sensibly that I had no option as I wasn't in a position to pack in the game. I was just a working man like everyone else. So back I went and I concede that my mood was bitter.

It was a difficult time for the family, too. The older girls had settled into jobs and didn't want to go to Manchester. So we decided to buy them a small flat at King's Park in Glasgow. But this split the family. Both Liz and I missed the girls badly and it was two years before all the family moved down to join us.

The first year was very hard. I put my heart and soul into City, who had no money and had to let players go because they couldn't afford their wages. They were still in a state of shock after the big-spending eras of Malcolm Allison and John Bond. I appointed Jimmy Frizzell, a fellow Scot, as my assistant and was glad of his local knowledge. He had been manager of Oldham and knew the Manchester scene well. This was important.

Jimmy and I were left with so few players we sat for days on end thinking who we could get for as close to nothing as possible. City had horrendous debts in the wake of their halcyon spending-sprees on players. We could hardly buy a fish supper.

We pulled players out of our memories. Derek Parlane came on a free transfer from Leeds, Jim Tolmey from Lokeren in Belgium,

Heart and soul for City. Here I pose with Peter Swales.

and Neil McNab from Brighton. All three are Scots and we were accused of trying to turn Maine Road into Scotch Corner. I had remembered Tolmey with Morton, but was aware he could also be difficult to handle. We weren't in a position to be choosey. We got McNab from Brighton, where he had been a bit of a rebel, for around £25,000.

Tolmey's opening six months were fantastic. We went on a pre-season trip to West Germany and he was a revelation. In our opening League game at Crystal Palace in London he was also magnificent. McNab fitted in very well and all Parlane could do for six months was score goals but, unfortunately, later on his legs tired.

We were so short of players it was scarcely credible. We had to sell Tommy Caton to Arsenal for £450,000. He was a decent big lad and, apart from this, City couldn't afford to knock back any bid. I was able to buy Mick McCarthy from Barnsley for £200,000 as a result of the Caton deal and he did a great job. We needed a battler like him to give the side heart.

In the first season we would have scraped promotion but for Kevin Keegan. Chelsea and Sheffield Wednesday were the two best clubs in the Second Division and they went up deservedly. City would have joined them as the third team but for the work Keegan did for Newcastle United. Despite the presence of young Peter Beardsley, now of Liverpool, Keegan was the man who sparked Newcastle. His influence was immense.

There are very few players that I have greater respect for than Keegan, and this time, I'm referring only to his ability on the pitch. He was the heart and soul of Newcastle. It's a terrible thing to admit, but every time I read that Kevin had an injury I hoped it would keep him out of the Newcastle side for a game or two. Usually it didn't and I was glad in the end because I have such a high regard for him. He was certainly the difference between City and Newcastle. They had Keegan's inspirational qualities and we didn't.

In my second season at Maine Road we battled and battled. I remember 1 March because it's the day before my birthday. Liz had a surprise party for me and we beat Blackburn Rovers who hadn't lost at home for a couple of seasons. The win put City at the top of the League. We were going great but, as sometimes happens when a significant result is obtained, we lost a key player. Graham Baker, who was a big influence on the team, fell and dislocated his shoulder at Blackburn, so we had to do without his services at a vital period.

We made promotion in the third place with 74 points. Oxford (84) and Birmingham (82) were ahead of us. I will never forget the last game against Charlton at Maine Road. We had gone to Portsmouth and won 2-1 — a great result — and Mick McCarthy was outstanding with Paul Simpson also scoring an exceptional goal. But in our second last match we lost 3-2 to Notts County and a section of our fans got themselves into trouble for misbehaving.

On the final day, Huddersfield met Portsmouth at home. The position was that if we lost to Charlton and Portsmouth won they would get promotion and not us. My one consolation was that

Huddersfield were a fair side under Mick Buxton. City were brimming over with problems. I had no centre-half as McCarthy and Nicky Reid were suspended. I had to field a makeshift team. In fact, the side which won my only promotion-winning match was: Williams, Lomax, Power, May, Clements, Phillips, Simpson, McNab, Melrose, Tolmey, Kinsey.

City were up against it. I put on my best lightweight suit and swept into the ground early in the morning. Everyone was a bag of nerves. But that was the very reason I was there so early and looking, I hoped, a million dollars. I strode around exuding confidence, telling everyone who would listen that we would win and go to the First Division in season 1985-86. I felt this had been transmitted to the team and that was really all that bothered me.

We scored twice early on and eventually led 5-0 before Charlton got a consolation goal which jubilant City fans cheered as well. Our scorers were Andy May, Jim Melrose, Dave Phillips (2) and Paul Simpson. It was a tremendous achievement. There hadn't been so much excitement — or champagne! — at Maine Road for years.

In the following season, again we weren't in a position financially to do the strengthening which was required. The difference between the top divisions in England is very similar to moving up from the First to the Premier League in Scotland. It is a considerable jump. A club needs to be very lucky to have a young team which is developing positively or else complete restructuring is a must. The demands of the English First Division are so much greater than the Second that it is frightening.

I took Mark Lillas, from Huddersfield, and he was a really wholehearted centre-forward. I also obtained Irishman Sammy McIlroy on free transfer from Stoke because of his experience. This was the kind of transfer we had to arrange because we didn't have the cash to carry out a bigger deal.

We survived that season because of one spell in which we hoisted ourselves to tenth position. We went to White Hart Lane and beat Tottenham 2-0. But in the last part of the season we struggled. Although we found it hard to win a game we managed to stay in the First Division. When I look back it was a tremendous shoestring achievement, but I knew we had to tighten up for next season — or else!

Meanwhile we were having great success with our youth team.

Neil McNab and Jim Melrose were too of my City signings. Both featured in the promotion-winning side.

Directors of City with whom I'm still very friendly and the club secretary, Bernard Holford, kept telling me to be patient. Bernard was of the opinion that we had to keep cool and hope that the boys developed properly. City's kids won the FA Youth Cup, which is really big in England, in the club's first year back in the First Division. In fact, City are still pinning their hopes on youngsters because they can't afford to deal in the quality end of the transfer market. I think they now accept that it's the only way but that it will take time.

My fourth season at Maine Road kicked off with the usual problems of trying to be patient — difficult for me! — and dabbling on the cheap in the transfer market. The English First Division is demanding but at least clubs only have to meet twice as against four times in the Premier League. Every team in England is also full-time. Apart from the fact that we were always looking for bargain buys at Maine Road, we also had to persuade other clubs to accept payment on the never-never. I tried to convince the board that dealing like this, we would never get the players we really wanted.

Ian Ferguson, now with Rangers, was a youngster I fancied when he was still with Clyde. But we couldn't afford the £60,000 although now he is valued at around £1 million. I offered my ex-assistant and team-mate John Clark, the Shawfield manager, all kinds of build-up deals, but they wanted cash and I could understand their attitude. That was typical of the disappointments at the time.

I have a lot of time for Peter Swales and not a little admiration for him as chairman at Maine Road. I enjoyed my relationship with him and my family settled to love Manchester and the people. Mr Swales and I had regular meetings either in his office or mine. He insisted that I called him Peter. We always got on well. He assured me he was anxious to put City in the position of buying big again.

He took unbelievable flak and didn't flinch. He never walked away from anything, if people wanted to criticise he was prepared to meet them face to face. He has been portrayed in many ways, but I have an unshakeable liking and respect for him. He is a good chairman and would be even better in sounder financial circumstances. I certainly learned from him and I don't mind admitting it.

I met a group of fans with Mr Swales shortly after I went to Manchester. I was impressed by the way he handled them. He admitted frankly he had made mistakes in the past, and had agreed to spend fortunes which turned out to be bad business. "I can't do anything about the past," he said, "but I'm doing my best to remedy things in the future." His candour went down well. The supporters were impressed by his sincerity and so was I.

City had a board of 12 out of necessity. They all made contributions to keep the club going. The feeling for the club was great. Some of the directors put in as much as £100,000. I didn't feel I was under any pressure — at least, not until they appointed Freddie Pye as vice-chairman while I was on holiday.

He was given the title of Director in Charge of Team Affairs, which I thought was ominous. I never had a relationship with Mr Pye. After his appointment there was a lot of murmuring in the background and this sowed the seed for my move to Aston Villa.

Peter Swales didn't want me to go. Here he listens while I make a point.

The chairman tried to encourage me to get together with Mr Pye, but I couldn't bring myself to do it. He appeared to be working against me in team matters. Maybe I could have made a bigger effort, but I felt it was a bad appointment and Freddie Pye wanted to dictate policy.

For instance, I needed a striker but we couldn't afford to buy one. It turned out that Mr Pye and Ken Bates, of Chelsea, are friendly, so I was coerced into taking Gordon Davies from Stamford Bridge. The never-never deal worked out was nothing short of astonishing. When we met the player he had to phone his wife every five minutes or so to put points to her. Eventually, he left saying he didn't want to sign. But later he changed his mind. As a player, Davies had ability but wasn't prepared to be in on the

131

action. I didn't consider Gordon was a strong character either.

All this was making me think carefully about my position. I was impatient for success and probably had been spoiled in this respect at Celtic Park. I wanted their kind of triumphs. Rightly or wrongly people with ambition seek a platform where this is possible. So when Aston Villa's chairman, Doug Ellis, made overtures I was in the mood to listen.

City had played only seven of their 42 League matches when I left in that season, 1986-87, and handed over to Jimmy Frizzell. Of these seven we won one, drew four and lost two. So it wasn't exactly disaster form but, unhappily, City finished the season being relegated. This has been blamed on me. However, Jimmy himself pointed out that there was ample time after I had departed to push City up the table. His players were unable to make it and the bottom-line reason was lack of cash.

Peter Swales didn't want me to go and he also thought Villa weren't right for me. However, upsetting influences in the background at Maine Road weren't going away. And, coming back from the World Cup finals at Mexico, I also felt I was a prime contender for the Scottish job which Alex Ferguson was giving up after taking it on part-time following the sudden death of Jock Stein. Expectations about Scotland turned out to be another disappointment. With the benefit of hindsight I often wonder why I made the decision to go to Villa. On reflection the offer came at a time when things were low for me, combined with the feeling that somebody wasn't working in my favour on the board. It made me vulnerable.

Villa were on their uppers when Graeme Turner was sacked. Incidentally, he said I was the man to succeed him. He thought he was doing me a favour, but it turned out quite the reverse. The club were at the bottom of the First Division and nothing was going right for them. In seven League matches their only victory was 2-1 against Luton. I spoke to several prominent people and the advice was to keep clear of Villa and Doug Ellis. However, I wasn't happy with the City set-up so, for the first time in my life, I was motivated by money. I was promised all kinds of things. Cash has never been an overriding issue for me and this was the one time I let it seriously influence my thinking.

A difficulty with Mr Ellis is that he can be complex, forgetful and inconsistent. Liz came with me to his house to discuss the job and later she was as appalled as me over his failure to keep promises and his ability to twist what had been agreed. What he told us that night was quickly forgotten.

He said, for example, that he appreciated that Villa were down, but he indicated there would be ample funds available to help rectify this. This wasn't true. One of the first things I received was a memo — Mr Ellis always sent memos — giving a projected budget which indicated that the club had no option but to sell a player. Steve Hodge was the one to go, for £650,000 to Spurs. The player wanted a move as he felt playing for a club in relegation trouble wouldn't do his England chances any good. I found Hodge a reasonable bloke who didn't cause any trouble and worked hard at his game. However, the Villa fans didn't seem to fancy him.

I was aware that going to Villa in September 1986 was a gamble. I also fell for a lot of the guff that Doug Ellis talked. On top of this I hoped, but never really believed, that I would end up back with Celtic. Going to a club with a chairman like Mr Ellis it is necessary to have a watertight contract. I encouraged a get-out clause which provided for a pay-out of £25,000. When I left Villa I had difficulty getting considerably less than that. It was six or seven weeks before Mr Ellis was even interested in talking to my accountant, Frank Walker. Meanwhile stories were circulating that I had been paid £75,000, and I could only guess where they originated.

We had a good string of results when I joined Villa at first. I thought we were starting to turn the corner. In the Littlewoods Cup we drew 1-1 away with Reading and then beat them 4-1 at home. However, I should have analysed why Villa were at the bottom. We won 2-0 against Charlton on Boxing Day. For the remainder of the season we had only two other victories. Our highest League scorer was defender Alan Evans with six — all from penalties. It is significant that Graham Taylor, my successor from Watford, had a clear-out. That's what I should have insisted on doing. We also suffered abnormally from injuries and this contributed more than somewhat to our slide.

Mr Ellis is a well-paid chief executive of the club. I was never tempted to call him Doug. It was surprising how easy it was for players to by-pass the manager and speak to him directly. He openly encouraged them talking to him. If I was having trouble with a player he seemed to go to the chairman's office as a matter of course to pour out his grievances. There was no doubt in my mind as well that Mr Ellis wanted to influence the choice of players and who would join the club. Before my time he apparently flew to Portugal to sign Andy Gray who was on holiday there. He claimed this was with the authority of the manager.

I quickly made enemies in the dressing-room at Villa Park. This was not something that particularly upset me, but when such a situation arises a manager needs the confidence of his board, and particularly the chairman, to be left to deal as he sees fit. Unfortunately, he continued to like players coming to him. I have no doubt that Mr Ellis heard plenty about me in this way. To be fair too, I had been warned that this tittle-tattle was par for the course before I took the job.

However, I cannot avoid saying that I found Mr Ellis absolutely impossible. There's no way I could have gone on indefinitely. He even twisted basic things. I made it clear from the start that I wouldn't move my family from Manchester immediately because I didn't want to interrupt Martyn's schooling at that point. He agreed that we would change over at the end of the first season. He then turned this round into an allegation that I didn't want to live in Birmingham.

Very early on Mr Ellis was apparently talking to other managers about Villa and there were hints even then that I was for the boot. There were stories that Ron Atkinson would take over and a friend of his confided at a party that this could be true — if Big Ron wanted it. I frequently challenged Mr Ellis about the source of this information but he denied that he had any knowledge of the rumours that were going around. He once asked if I was calling him a liar. What a pity I wasn't in a position to give an honest answer.

What I wanted to do more than anything was to keep Villa in the First Division. Then I would have walked away from the job. I knew that Mr Ellis was talking behind my back because friends told me about conversations with him. Again I challenged him to be frank with me but I don't think he understands what this means.

Oddly, perhaps the best thing that happened to Villa was going to the Second Division. It gave them the scope and the opportunity to change the staff in the way that was necessary. I told Mr Ellis and his co-directors at a board meeting that what was needed was a major clear-out. I warned the directors this would have to be done. There was no way ahead unless there was a clear-out. Personnel at every level in the club had to go, including youths. I had appointed a new chief scout as a start but, fighting for our lives in the First Division, it was not the time to pull the place asunder. The fact that such an upheaval was necessary merely confirmed to me the influence Mr Ellis had in the signings of my predecessors.

When I left Villa after only eight months my sacking was forecast in a morning tabloid. This riled me. Football managers are like everyone else. We have feelings and so do our families. If we are not doing our job, then it is right for the boss to come along, say so, and take the necessary action. The manner in which I was removed by Villa was annoying, but I should have expected it. We had only one game to go and that was against Manchester United.

The day before, after reading my fate in the paper, I went to the training ground as usual. I was always there around nine o'clock, which made a nonsense of the manufactured criticism that I didn't spend enough time in Birmingham. I never left until late and, if there was a game or a special function, I stayed overnight. It was rubbish to say I wasn't spending enough time at the club. I left Manchester every morning at seven thirty and enjoyed it because I'm an early bird by inclination. The drive on the motorway also gave me time to think and produce ideas.

Mr Ellis tried to wheel and deal. I felt he orchestrated a situation where he wanted to sell young England defender Tony Dorigo, who is very talented. I was asked at a board meeting what my reaction would be if Chelsea came on about Dorigo. I said we'd have to tell them we weren't interested in selling unless we could do a reasonable deal with David Speedie. We needed somebody with Speedie's ability and attitude at that time. The chairman persisted and asked again what I would do if Ken Bates made an offer for Dorigo with no strings attached. I said I would reject it. At that very moment, right on cue as it were, the phone rang. Mr Ellis picked it up, made a face, then covered the mouthpiece to say: "You won't believe who this is. It's Ken Bates." I was expected to swallow that the Chelsea chairman had called during a board meeting by pure coincidence. Obviously, the Villa chairman had set the thing up knowing full well that Bates would phone when he did.

I never had a chance at Villa and should never have taken the job. However, back at Celtic Park, I am scarred by what went on at Birmingham but I'm much wiser because of it. Nor does criticism worry me as much because I have the belief in myself to go on regardless and do the things which I feel are necessary. I'm a strong person and the experience south of the border has made me a better manager. While I regret the Villa episode I've regarded it like a University course in soccer management. Indeed, I found out a lot of things that no lecturer could ever have told me.

Villa's record was not good during my term. An acute shortage of cash and injuries to players knocked us sideways. I hardly ever saw the former Aberdeen midfielder Neale Cooper when he was fit or, for that matter, Mark Walters, who has done well since moving to Rangers. We tallied 36 points which didn't please me at all. At home that season Villa won seven games, drew seven and lost seven which at least shows a degree of consistency! Away we had only one victory, drawing five and losing 15.

Mr Ellis had the uncanny knack, when others were feeling a bit vulnerable, of throwing salt into an open wound. For instance, he would stroll into the dressing-room after a drawn or losing game and say something like: "Oh, dearie, dearie me, that's more points lost." As if anybody needed reminding.

I eventually tried to sign David Speedie but, whereas Dorigo agreed Chelsea's terms, Villa couldn't come up to what Speedie's agent stipulated. David was under a bit of a cloud at Stamford Bridge, but he still wanted any move to be worthwhile. I was impressed chatting to Speedie and would have liked to sign him for Villa. He was what we needed . . . a powerhouse on the pitch. But David wanted a London-type contract and Villa couldn't afford it.

My sojourn in England was plagued by one common factor — a shortage of money at both Manchester City and Aston Villa. In the right circumstances, and given enough time, it is possible to survive and rebuild. I was required to do both these things immediately and on a shoestring. It was asking the impossible.

It is baloney to suggest that a manager schooled in Scotland can't succeed in England. The trick is to avoid a Citadel of Doom like Villa and a chairman in the mould of Doug Ellis. I was delighted, by the way, when Villa won promotion to the First Division again and I wish them luck.

Making a speech and proud in my kilt at the Celtic Centenary Dinner in Glasgow's Albany Hotel.

In my mood of despair after being sacked for the first — and, I hope, last — time in my career I was cheered by the fact that I wasn't exactly unwanted. Within a few days of Villa booting me I had a big-money offer to go to the Middle East and I was given some very good advice by Dave Mackay. However, I decided to take my chances at home as I didn't want to split up the family again.

Then Airdrie came on the scene with a splendid offer which I pondered long and hard. Since they were good enough to consider me I felt they were due a bit of respect in return. I went to Broomfield and met their officials but, in the end, I felt it wasn't for me. There seemed no point in taking a job if I wasn't 100 per cent enthusiastic about it. This would have been cheating and that is not my style.

A long time before this, in October 1984, while I was with Manchester City, Hibs made me a good offer to return to Scotland. Hibs have always been a club who appealed to me. I remember in my schooldays seeing Motherwell playing them at Fir Park in the Scottish Cup. "The Famous Five" forward line were on show — Gordon Smith, Bobby Johnstone, Lawrie Reilly, Eddie Turnbull and Willie Ormond — and they slaughtered Motherwell. Memories such as this linger on so the offer did have an appeal and, at the time, my three oldest girls — Susan, Carol and Libby — were still living in Glasgow. Kenny Waugh, the Hibs chairman, offered a very good contract but, in the end, I felt I had to stay loyal to City. When I think of what Alex MacDonald and Sandy Jardine have achieved at Hearts it would certainly have been a good challenge at Easter Road. But my friendship with Peter Swales was the deciding factor. I would have felt guilty leaving him, which makes it all the more ironic that I did later on.

Again, at the end of the season in which Manchester City clinched promotion the Spanish club Real Sociedad approached me, saying they wanted to change their approach and run the club on British lines. Would I like the job? I had taken Celtic to San Sebastian in 1982 and, though we lost 3-2 on aggregate, they liked the way I organised things and wanted me to join them. In many ways it appealed to me and especially as I speak Spanish reasonably well. But the fact that City had just won promotion to the First Division really meant I couldn't leave. Sociedad then came back with a short list of names and asked whom I

Liz and I celebrate our winning ways.

recommended. John Toshack was among the names and I said he was their man. I'm not saying John got the job because of me but I'm certainly glad he has done so well.

Chapter Nine

The Media and Me

EVER since my playing days I have enjoyed good relations with the Press. I haven't always agreed with what they have written and sometimes I've told them so. Maybe we've fallen out for a day or two but that's been it. I try to understand their job as well as my own. On foreign trips I spend a reasonable amount of time with the Press in the belief that they have a part to play. I also like to know what's going on among them and how they are thinking.

With all this in mind and a 6-0 victory over the Hungarian team Diosgyeori in the first round of the Cup Winners' Cup at Parkhead on 20 August 1980, I thought we were going for a relaxed trip in the return leg. Hungary is one of the pleasanter places behind the Iron Curtain. It would have been nice to spend a few days in Budapest, the Paris of the Eastern Bloc, but there was no time for that. Since we were not chartering a plane it meant a trip by shuttle to London, from there to Budapest and then on by coach to Diosgyeori. I never think this is the ideal way for a team to travel because so many things can wrong.

Three days after our runaway first-leg victory in the Cup Winners' Cup we lost 2-1 to Rangers at Parkhead because of a goal scored 30 seconds from the end by Alex Miller. It was disappointing for our fans and I fully appreciate this. However, I also considered that getting to the second round of the second most important European competiton would be some consolation. So it was in this frame of mind that I, and most of the rest of the party, set off for London and an overnight stay at the Excelsior Hotel, near Heathrow Airport.

Harry Hood seems to think the joke's on me because I have my bunnet on! This was February 1974.

Once the players have gone to bed it is quite normal for officials and the Press to mingle in the lounge or at the bar. There is usually a bit of banter and it's all part of having good relations between football and the people who write about it.

I sat with a group of half-a-dozen reporters and some of the directors were at a nearby table discussing football with others who were in our party. Gerry McNee, whom I always regarded as being a fan of Celtic, began to criticise our players, alleging indiscipline in the Old Firm match. What he said surprised me. He was also quite aggressive and eventually I made it clear I wasn't prepared to accept that kind of talk at a friendly late-night get-together. None in the party were even remotely "tired and emotional". Words became stronger until Mr McNee, then writing for the *Star* but now for its sister paper the *Daily Express*, said to me: "You and I had better go outside and settle this."

Whatever part of the world you come from the suggestion means only one thing. Stupidly, because the argument had become heated, out I went. Let me make it abundantly clear that I made an error of judgment. I should not have become involved and would never ever do so again. It was against all good sense and my natural inclination.

Mr McNee was just ahead of me as we went down a wide, sloping corridor. He turned towards me and I thought he was going to have a go. I decided in an instant to retaliate first and aimed a blow which hit him on the cheekbone. The ring on my finger aggravated the damage which was really only slight although at the time it was bleeding. There was only one blow, thank goodness. Mr McNee was on all fours and covering his head when a couple of his colleagues came running towards us. I realised in a flash what an idiot I was.

The following day, after a sleepless night, I realised I had to make a move. I called the newspaper party together at the airport and said frankly that I had been wrong and assured them that nobody's job would be made difficult because of what had gone on. I added that I hoped it wouldn't spoil the trip for anyone as it should never have happened — and I wished sincerely that it hadn't. The responsibility was mine and I didn't seek to blame anybody else. I remember very clearly saying: "I apologise to you all — and that includes you, Gerry." I leant over to look at him as he was on the right hand side of the group.

To my surprise he replied quickly: "Can I shake your hand, big man?" That, I thought, would be the end of it. I had made my apology and admitted I was wrong. With my mining background apologies don't come easily. Imagining it was over was, however, wishful thinking.

We lost the game 2-1 but went through on a 7-2 aggregate so there was no hassle there. Let me say that in my career in football I've seen loads of two-minute fights. It happens regularly in training. That's the nature of the game. But it's never allowed to carry on. Contestants quickly laugh about it and it becomes a joke for a few days. But that's all. Naïvely, I thought this would happen with my particular one-punch "battle" and particularly as I had publicly eaten humble pie.

I spoke to the Celtic chairman about the incident and he said he appreciated the fact that I had explained my side to him. He counselled that we should wait to see what happened. I began to be confident the incident had blown over because a month passed and there was no mention of it although there was a lot of gossip. The journalists on the trip had judged that, with no witness to vouch for what had gone on, the police not involved in any way, and Mr McNee at that stage denying anything had happened, there was no printable story.

Then, on Sunday 5 October, the incident exploded without warning on to the front pages. I felt terrible and particularly for my family. There were Press photographers outside my house and reporters were knocking on the door or phoning. I felt like a murder suspect or a train robber. It isn't pleasant having to jump over neighbours' walls to get away unseen from your own home.

I thought the circumstances of the story being published were strange. Only two people knew what had happened. It certainly wasn't me who talked. I am not suggesting Mr McNee went to a Sunday paper but they certainly had help from some source in gaining confirmation. In football and newspapers there are always plenty of people who are prepared to gossip and I had no shortage of inside information from many Press sources.

My father tried to take some of the worry out of my thinking. As an ex-soldier used to discipline he was well aware I was wrong, no matter the provocation, to lift my hands. But he still pointed out that it would be a seven-day wonder. Day and daily, he said, people do things when they are in a temper or when their passions are stoked high, so perhaps I had the incident out of proportion.

I offered my resignation to the chairman who rejected it. I was to repeat this in a second saga relating to the same reporter. However, despite this I was reprimanded and fined £500 at a board meeting. The decision was to be kept private but within a short time everybody knew that I had been rapped. Since I had never kidded the Press, nor favoured one section against the other, nor unfairly distributed news, it hurt me deeply that the matter was taken so far — after an apology had been given and apparently accepted.

When I reflected on the London hotel barney it occurred to me that the reason for it ran much deeper. Mr McNee had more interest in what I can only call the club's politics than other reporters. He was displeased when I allowed Johannes Edvaldsson to go to America and seemed to feel he was a better judge of a centre-half than me. He even phoned Edvaldsson in America and recorded an interview for radio.

The truth was that when I came back to Parkhead from Aberdeen the first person in my office was Edvaldsson — or "Shuggy" as we called him. He felt that he had been badly treated by Celtic because he believed that at the end of his contract he would be a free agent. This wasn't so. At the same time I received a host of phone calls from the Continent and America about "Shuggy" so there seemed to be no doubt that somebody was trying to move him on. He also wanted assistance to buy a pub in Glasgow, but later changed his mind.

Mr McNee made a thing about this and, when it came to the Scottish Cup final of 1980 against Rangers, I was left with Roddie MacDonald and Tom McAdam suspended. In addition, Jim Casey, who was to step in as the centre-half, went over on his ankle in a practice for Hampden. Mr McNee referred to the "short-sighted policy" which had led to Edvaldsson being allowed to go. Naturally, I felt strongly as the player had asked to be transferred. He wanted pastures new and had had enough of Celtic.

The irony was that we put Mike Conroy to centre-half in the final, won 1-0, and he was outstanding. It seemed that Mr McNee was interesting himself in team personalities very early in his career as a sportswriter in a way that more experienced, but still very critical, journalists don't seem to do.

Some time following the London hotel incident, and after we had been eliminated from the Cup Winners' Cup in Rumania, a group of reporters was outside the door of our dressing-room at Paisley after the match. I quickly noted that Mr McNee was among them and indicated that I wouldn't speak as long as he was there. This began another hoo-ha and there was a suggestion that I would be invited before the National Union of Journalists. I would have been pleased to meet them as I have always been a supporter of the trades union movement. The opportunity was not given to me, however.

Since I hadn't called a Press Conference I thought I had the basic right to decide to whom I would speak. At that time the club decided I was wrong although nowadays clubs have a different attitude. The Celtic board, in their wisdom, sent me a terse warning letter saying that I had to speak to reporters whether I liked it or not.

Sandwiched between the London incident and the scene at Paisley were our second round Cup Winners' Cup-ties. We had to go to Rumania after beating Politechnica Timisoara 2-1 at Parkhead with Charlie Nicholas scoring both goals. The return game was incredible and the Greek referee, Nicolas Iangvinus, was the worst I have ever seen. Roddie MacDonald was dismissed in the 17th minute along with the home goalie Moise. The Rumanian objected to Roddie trying to get in a shot and fouled him. Both players were sent off, which was farcical. Next Peter Latchford was blatantly fouled as he went for a cross from the right. Pushed by Paltinisan, Peter dropped the ball, which the Rumanian promptly shot into the net. The referee remarkably gave a goal. Then, late in the match, he sent off Frank McGarvey, who had already been booked, for arguing. I have never before or since seen such an awful display of match-handling. Even Greek newspapers criticised the referee's appointment to the tie because he had been involved in all sorts of trouble at home.

After the highly controversial match the Rumanians held a function in the hotel in which we were staying. And they were well aware of this as they fixed up our accommodation. The referee and the two linesmen were at the top table in an area which wasn't particularly private. Our players were openly listening to what was going on. Gerry McNee walked to the top table and remonstrated with the Greek about his refereeing. Not long after this the match official walked to a table at which some of our lads were sitting, grabbed McGarvey and accused him of all sorts of things. "You are the one who caused me all the trouble in the match," the referee told Frank.

I moved down the table to get McGarvey and the others out of the way to avoid trouble. Once everything had settled down and the players had gone to their rooms I went to see the chairman. And found Mr McNee in the room where he had already given his version of what had gone on. I made it very clear that I didn't expect him, or any other journalist, to go behind my back to report to the chairman. I then sat down and told the chairman everything I had seen, including the fact that Mr McNee had been speaking to the referee. I also made it clear that I felt he was being deliberately vindictive towards me, so I had no wish to speak to him in the future.

When we returned to Scotland I explained to the Celtic board and emphasised that I had no complaint against Mr McNee's paper, but I didn't wish to speak to him personally. It was following this that the situation arose at Paisley, but I can only say that I had made it clear to Mr McNee that I had no wish to speak to him.

More important, I felt the Greek referee panicked following the happenings in the hotel and came up with a cock-and-bull story involving John Clark, who was later banned from official UEFA functions for two years for "extremely grave insults to the referee". The club was fined £600 and MacDonald and McGarvey were each banned for three months. The penalties were described at the time as "among the toughest ever handed out". John Clark didn't deserve what he got and, although he appealed, the sentence stood. Celtic's complaint about the quality of refereeing was apparently ignored.

Since I returned to Parkhead as manager for the second time I have told Mr McNee that I will supply him with information regarding the club, but both of us know that we will never be good friends. He has rarely contacted me since.

I have very good relations with the rest of the media. I am pretty sure of that — they voted me Manager of the Year for a second

146

The Celtic bench, absorbed to a man.

time. It is an honour which I cherish highly and I also recall that I was the first-ever Player of the Year nominated by the Scottish Football Writers' Association at their annual dinner 'way back in 1965.

The Press corps have, naturally, changed quite a lot since I first got to know them. The attitude of papers to items they report has also been dramatically revised. I am not sure it is for the better but it is not for me to judge. What I am repeating is that I recognise the importance of good publicity for the game and I will continue to work to try to steer as much of this as possible towards Celtic and the Scottish game generally.

Chapter Ten

Whistling While They Work

I SYMPATHISE with referees because they are involved as part-timers — paid a mere £60 for a League game — in a professional sport where often their actions can be interpreted by so many as being almost as important as life or death. Because of the tension and the cut-throat aspect of football, and professional sport in general, the referee must make decisions which can influence people's livelihoods. It is all very well to say contestants should always behave in a totally composed and rational manner, but quite often the people who say or write these things don't act in the same manner themselves in much less difficult situations.

There is a general forgetfulness that football is an explosive sport which has physical contact as an integral part of the play. Emotions are often high. So it can be difficult to be cool and calm all the time, desirable though this might be. I wonder, in fact, about people who show no signs of emotion. Do they have the necessary passion for professional sport?.

TV sports presentations are now so sophisticated that a referee can be embarrassed by a slow-motion re-run of an incident which shows him to be wrong. The referee, who has to make an instant decision, does not have the advantage of studying moves on the video before making up his mind. Just as players are human, so are the whistlers. They can make mistakes like everyone else. What they have to hope is that when they blunder the situation is not crucial and as few as possible see it.

There is not enough communication between referees, managers and players. I don't think sending a referee to talk to players at the ground is the right way to solve this. Rather than have formal meetings referees should be encouraged to be open and frank with players and officials and mix with them when the opportunity presents itself.

I don't think full-time referees would improve judgments, but when I am told that the man in charge of the Cup final is paid only £100 I wonder when we will realise their importance and reward them properly. I would be against it, but full-time refereeing would certainly make officials fitter and that is an area which needs improvement. Some are in peak condition, but there are others who are less than fit. I'm aware that they have to do physical tests, but in the modern-day game the general standard of fitness needs to be improved.

Referees should be encouraged to show their personalities. Tom Wharton, now an SFA supervisor and highly regarded by FIFA, the world's governing body, maximised his presence and personality to the best advantage. He was an outstanding referee. A lot of current referees develop into sergeant-major types. So many fine whistlers in the past were respected for being themselves. Jack Mowat, the long-time chairman of the supervisors who handled the 1960 European Cup final between Real Madrid and Eintracht, which the Spaniards won 7-3, had stature which ensured respect from even world-known players. And, by the way, he was paid 18 pence in expenses for handling the match — with no fee — although 135,000 saw a great spectacle at Hampden. As a youngster I remember Mr Mowat as pretty fearsome, but he didn't send off or caution willy-nilly. Laws must be applied, but referees should also call on the unwritten Law 18 which is commonsense. More freedom, a good deal more, should be afforded so that they can demonstrate individuality.

A referee should be allowed, in special circumstances, to speak to a player after he has been yellow-carded rather than be regimented into sending him off for a trivial second offence. The rule for referees is that they can speak to a player once, then if necessary show him the yellow card. Next they have to send him off if they have to speak to him again for an offence. In exceptional cases the match official should be given leeway in these matters.

For example, in a Celtic-Rangers match at Parkhead in August 1969, FIFA-listed Jim Callaghan's linesman drew attention to an incident involving Willie Johnston and John Hughes. The Celt had already been booked. Mr Callaghan decided to have a word with Big John and for this the referee was suspended for two months. Once he decided to speak to the player a second time he had to send him off, whereas I argue his commonsense should have been supported. I considered the punishment severe and felt that the SFA overreacted to a complaint from Rangers.

Fouls should be looked at in the context of the game. Most fouls are committed accidentally although the governing word is intention. However, I must say there is far too much play-acting on the pitch. At one time we laughed at the Continentals when they rolled about apparently near to death but recovered miraculously with a wipe of the sponge. We are just as bad now. I wonder if players have lost respect for their fellow professionals. Gamesmanship has always been a part of football but now certain players seem keen, maybe even desperate, to get an opponent into trouble.

One thing I am sure of — the game is not as physical as it was. There are more dramatic actions and stupid fouls but it's not as hard as it was in my day. But consistency in refereeing decisions is important. I don't think there is enough of it. Failure to penalise identical offences in the same way riles players.

I think Brian McGinlay has been the best referee in recent times in Scotland. It was unfortunate he resigned just before the World Cup in Mexico where he was due to officiate. He is back this season and I am pleased about that. Kenny Hope uses his personality to a greater degree than others, and I felt Alan Ferguson was forced to retire too soon. He was fit and could have been allowed to go on. Too many top referees leave the game prematurely. Each official should be judged on his ability and fitness and not retired automatically on reaching an age barrier. Mr Ferguson always maintained a high physical standard. I don't think he should have been forced to quit at 50. It's like saying every player should go at 35. The principle is the same. It was disappointing to see him departing the scene as he did. Referees are very much like goalkeepers. They mature with age in the later stages of their career. The 50 mark can be too young for many. They may well be at their peak because they are harnessing all their experience.

Another referee I like is George Smith, from Edinbugh, who handled the Scottish Cup final when we beat Dundee United.

Eyeball-to-eyeball with referee Andrew Waddell. It's a moment I would rather forget.

Sometimes he applies the laws too strictly, but he is an excellent referee. Bob Valentine, who retires at the end of the 1988-89 season, is a credit to the whistling business and I am not surprised he is so highly thought of by UEFA, the European ruling body.

In the modern game I also feel too much responsibility is given to linesmen. The offside law is much maligned. A player is judged to be onside or offside at the moment the ball is played forward. But linesmen are flagging players offside when the ball is either in flight or has reached its destination.

Continental referees are better at applying the advantage law. They take a fraction of a second to judge if there is something to be gained by allowing play to run on when a foul has been committed. Giving the advantage is better than stopping the game constantly. If the flow of the game is stopped too often it loses its appeal to the spectators. The type of football Celtic play, and the brand I encourage, suffers when play is held up too often for free-kicks. There is, of course, the unkind suggestion that a free-kick gives a referee a wee break in a hectic match!

I have found Continentals less rigid in their application of the laws. The best referees, in my experience, come from West Germany and Holland. I felt much more secure travelling for a big European match with either a German or a Dutchman in the middle. They seemed able to bridge the British and Continental styles successfully. The Dutch, if anything, are less rigid than the Germans and are a cavalier people whom I like very much away from football. I always thought Charles Corver was a very good referee. In fact, I would pick him out as the best.

I was sent off twice in my career. The first time was at East Stirling, then in the old 18-club First Division, and the second during a tour game in Bermuda. Each time I was trying to protect team-mates in my capacity as captain. In the East Stirling game Stevie Chalmers and Jake McQueen, a left-back of the Falkirk team, got involved in several incidents. I thought Stevie was being unfairly treated. This is where referees sometimes read a situation wrongly. Sensible players do not side with a team-mate if he is in the wrong. I intervened to back up Stevie and was sent off. In these circumstances referees create problems for themselves. Players aren't daft. They see injustices and won't put up with them for ever.

Two orderings-off in a long career was not too bad.

I was shocked to be ordered off in Bermuda, because it was in a friendly tour match which we were winning easily. However, the local referee was adamant and, I suppose, red-carding me gave him status. A local player took a swinging kick at Jimmy Quinn, by no means the first, and I protested. I am not condoning what I did in either case, but the experience was part of the process of growing up as a footballer. Two orderings-off in a long career as a centre-half may not seem a bad record, but I'm not proud that I went for stupid reasons. I have no sympathy with myself. Sitting across the table in judgment I would have come down very, very hard.

I have been in trouble, too, as a manager simply because I couldn't stop myself becoming involved in the tensions of matches. It is easy to say responsible people shouldn't do this, but the pressures on managers are at times horrendous. In England I took a conscious decision to view games more objectively from the dug-out. It hasn't worked entirely because any manager or coach who can sit on his backside and not react to some things must be . . . well, a very unusual person. Franz Beckenbauer, the manager of

153

West Germany, is an exception. He stands up during games and shows little, if any, emotion. However, the German outlook is a bit different from ours.

The worst incident in which I was involved occurred in November 1982. Against Aberdeen I thought a third goal by Mark McGhee, then a Dons player, was offside. In fact, we lost 3-1. My players considered the referee had been inconsistent, although others may not have agreed. Danny McGrain had been sent off and the Dons had scored the first goal from a disputed penalty.

It is difficult to make a formal protest because managers are not allowed to say anything. So an impulsive challenge from the track is occasionally made — rash though it may be. I found myself in an eyeball-to-eyeball confrontation with referee Andrew Waddell in full view of the crowd. I could have jumped back into the dug-out and might have escaped censure, but I decided I had to make an issue. I was sorry afterwards. It was an error of judgment. I let the fans and the players down. My dignity also took a dent and I regretted the confrontation very much.

The referee issued a formal caution and ordered me to the stand. There was no great exchange of words. He was doing his job as he saw it. I was fined £200 and severely reprimanded. The hearing by the Disciplinary Committee was fair and I had no complaints about their "sentence".

However, I am bound to say that sometimes the SFA treat club officials like errant schoolboys. They are too concerned about reading little paragraphs in newspapers which many haven't even noticed and turning the issue into a mini-witchhunt. I feel more public dialogue should be allowed. Football is a game which thrives on debate. Managers and coaches are too often asked to explain insignificant quotes.

And surely it is also wrong to deny a referee the right to speak? He is not irresponsible. I don't think referees would hit out dramatically if they were allowed — as they are in England — to speak if they see fit. By gagging referees, officialdom seems to be saying that they can't be trusted to express themselves properly. But there are times when they should be allowed to explain a decision without getting into an argument. It would limit trouble. If this silent treatment stays, the game will continue to have problems. We need to understand each other's jobs much better.

There is no reason why this can't be achieved.

It is claimed that rugby is more sporting and that football should lift some of its ideas. The important difference is that rugby is an amateur game, so the livelihoods of players are not affected by what happens on the field. The rugby rules are also clearer and, apart from internationals, the tension big crowds create is not a factor. I think comparing the two games is like saying boxing and wrestling are the same.

While I agree that managers should try to help a young referee I can never understand why there is not a more explicit grading system. In recent years, Grade I officials have, it's true, been eased into the bigger games. But I would like to see a panel of officials for each division with promotion and relegation in the same style as the clubs. It seems crazy to have a referee handling Celtic against Rangers one week and then refereeing at Stranraer or Alloa the next. It is unrealistic to say that all games are of equal importance. If there was a group of referees specifically for the Premier League the others would set this standard as their target.

One set-back is the number of times referees have to handle the same clubs in a League of ten. In bigger countries this doesn't occur but I still feel familiarity is preferable to inexperience. I also think it isn't a good idea to give the same Cup referee the replay. I know this has always been the habit and the reason is continuity. But incidents can occur which will still be uppermost in a referee's mind in a second match. I would rather have a fresh man.

For me the autocratic man in the middle never succeeded. Being treated like a schoolboy annoys players. One of the big names during my playing career was Bobby Davidson, who is now the chairman of Airdrie. He was highly thought of by FIFA as well as the SFA, but I personally felt he was too dismissive in his manner and that he gave the impression he was better than the teams he was refereeing.

It is vital to have high-quality referees. We tend to underplay their importance. If the game flows and the referee is inconspicuous this is ideal. But we must accept that it's not only the responsibility of the referee. Managers and players have a common interest with referees to promote football. We must get together, talk about the problems and try to discover ways of finding solutions.

Chapter Eleven

The International Scene

BEING a manager at international level has always interested me because it means dealing with the best players in the country in games which are important to everyone. In fact, I was offered the Republic of Ireland job which Jack Charlton took over so successfully in February 1986. Around the same time Scotland sounded me out secretly about my availability.

I was with Manchester City and told Irish officials, in the first place, that becoming their manager was a possibility but the proper approaches had to be made through the club. Peter Swales eventually gave me permission to talk to them. The Irish FA felt that I could do the job part-time as most of their players were with English clubs, which put me in an ideal position to know their current form.

I then had a long discussion with the Maine Road chairman and couldn't do anything else but agree that it would be impractical to try to run City and the Republic team. The best manager in the world, with the best team in the world, would have difficulty dividing his time between international and club football. I also reckoned the right decision was not to take it on a part-time basis. It is difficult to do two jobs successfully. Once you embark on football management you give your body and soul to it. Everything else becomes secondary. There can be no diversions. Every thinking minute must be devoted to football and to organisation.

I was also offered the Irish job on a full-time basis and I was very flattered. The idea appealed to me, perhaps for the reason that although I was with a big club, it didn't now have the resources to return to the status it once had. In addition, I wasn't operating with top-quality players and this caused me personal frustrations. I was busily engaged trying to keep City out of trouble at the bottom end of the League instead of challenging at the top as I wanted to do.

The one thing which finally prevented me going to Ireland was that a new Scottish manager was to be appointed after the World Cup in Mexico. I had been sounded out by a high-ranking Scottish official before Scotland set out for South America under Alex Ferguson. I was asked about my contract situation with City, so I took it that the SFA had some interest in giving me the job.

I asked the SFA official if being the manager of Eire would prejudice my chances with Scotland. The reply was that it could very well do so. He also told me that paying compensation for a manager was not SFA policy. But if Scotland had moved for me, I'm sure I could have come to an arrangement with City about my release.

What was said on the telephone was another influencing factor in turning Ireland down. However, so many things have worked in my favour, including my short but disastrous spell with Aston Villa, that I can have no complaint. I wonder if the Parkhead job would have become available had I joined the SFA? I have no way of knowing. So my earlier disappointment was more than adequately balanced by my return to Celtic.

When I went to Mexico it was to comment on matches for TV but I used the trip to look at other countries and study the methods of other managers. I went to training sessions and Press conferences to see the different ways they were handled. It was quite illuminating and, at the time, I thought it would be useful if Scotland appointed me. I felt very confident I would be considered if a short list was drawn up. The Press are quite often very knowledgeable in matters concerning football jobs and they seemed sure this one was mine. However, I felt it wise to wait and see.

When I came home from Central America there was no encouraging phone call and eventually I went to Spain on holiday. While I was there my daughter Carol took a phone call at our home in Manchester from a TV journalist asking if I would be back in time for an SFA announcement which was to be made. As it happened I was travelling back on that day but I had no plans to be in Glasgow. The TV man had his answer and must have quickly realised it was not me who was to be the new Scotland boss.

I was disappointed. Like most people I was surprised that Andy Roxburgh had been promoted to run the team as well as continuing as Director of Coaching. However, I quite sincerely wished Andy well and I have tried to be helpful to him. I recognised that the Scotland job was difficult. Graeme Souness had retired, Kenny Dalglish was heading in his own direction and Gordon Strachan, who I thought was Scotland's best player in Mexico, was no longer such a great influence. A major transitional period was ahead. Andy's task was a big one. Scotland were lucky to get to Mexico. We were very fortunate in Iceland and in Wales, but although luck always plays a part, the team lacked the panache of previous sides in the finals. When players like Souness go, and others of similar class diminish, it is necessary to refashion the set-up completely.

We are fortunate in the qualifying games for the finals of the World Cup in Italy in 1990, in that we have been drawn in a group of five countries because it means two go forward. This is a break. France are not the team they were in Mexico or before that in the European Championships because of the loss of several great players such as Michel Platini. But they will still be very hard to beat. Cyprus and Norway should not really be good enough but Yugoslavia will pose problems, although I don't think in recent times they've ever been as good as their reputation. Every now and then Yugoslavia threaten to be a leading international team but I don't think they've ever achieved it.

Andy is an excellent coach. He has been coaching with boys and youth players and has done fine work. But it is inevitable that professionals will question the fact that he has no managerial experience at club level. He hasn't worked with seasoned professionals and I feel this is a necessary experience for a national manager.

He can compensate for managerial inexperience by his whole-hearted commitment to football, of which he is an avid student as well as being a good organiser. He is also a splendid man and nobody will work harder. He will do his utmost to bring about a resurgence in Scottish international football.

Of course, an advantage is that he has known a lot of the players — like Paul McStay — since they were in the youth sides and they

Paul McStay's influence at international level has got to be as great as it is for Celtic.

will have a rapport with him because of this. The experienced player is a bit different to handle from the enthusiastic, open-faced youth on the way up. Footballers develop their own opinions and attitudes and these can be difficult to dislodge.

Scots will need to be patient. Andy has a lot of looking and developing to do among the players coming up before he settles on a new team. Paul McStay's influence at international level has got to be as great as it is for Celtic. This may be asking a lot of a youngster but in the next year or so I see him being able to achieve that kind of authority. The part he played in Celtic's success was quite dramatic. If he can do it for Scotland it will be splendid. But he must go into the central midfield area with players who complement him.

Roy Aitken has played predominantly in central midfield but I disagree with this. Roy's best position is at the back and that's where he was such a key player for Celtic last season. The fact that we lost fewer goals than any Celtic team since 1925 indicates that Roy is in his true position. His influence, like Paul's, was enormous. Andy must find a combination in midfield with Paul given his head as the controller.

Ian Durrant of Rangers is another young midfielder whose influence will increase with experience and growing stature. He will be important in the Scotland set-up because he is genuinely skilful. It is not easy for Andy. Players aren't falling out of trees. Gordon Strachan can still be an asset, and Andy seems to agree with this. I know Strachan as a supreme professional and he can still do something for Scotland. The world is full of first-class players who are well into their thirties. We have an attitude in Scotland that immediately players hit 30 they are veterans. This is nonsense. Strachan's influence could still be considerable.

What worries me about Scotland, even going back to Mexico, is that we appear to have lost our dynamic pride and aggressive nature. We are copying the Continentals too much. I don't for one minute think we can go out and fire from the hip or tear into opponents. We've got to curb our aggression, but we must never lose it. We've gone too far towards the Continental way. They used to fear our attitude and appetite. We must get this spirit back and ally it to the experience and knowledge which is important to be successful at European and world level.

Roy Aitken's influence is enormous.

Players in this country are involved in too many competitive games, and this causes a problem for Andy Roxburgh as well as club managers. The possibility of him being able to pick all the players he wants is limited because of the increased chance of injury due to extra club commitments. This season the League is down to 36 games, which is a help. But look at the Continent where there are very few midweek games. In a country with our economic situation the fans also have a problem. They can't afford games in midweek and on a Saturday. We must think of them, too. The players don't have enough time to recover and practise between games and our customers are being asked to pay far too often.

There's nothing more clubs can do to help Scotland in the present set-up. Remember that success for me is about Celtic winning. Other managers feel the same way about their teams. Club football is our priority. The fans demand this as well. I would love to see an all-powerful Scottish side because I recognise the importance of this to the game, but it's not number one in my list of requirements.

There is a boom in the club game and we would like this continued into European competitions. The next thing is to have the success continued at international level. But that is the order of priorities. People say that the internationals should be given even more backing but, remember, the clubs are paying the high cost of signing and keeping good players. That's got to be recognised. I will always give whatever help I can to Scotland. If it doesn't handicap Celtic it's good for our players to be chosen. It assists their development.

Any manager moving into international football and imagining that he will be allowed to field every player he wants will find out quickly that he is sadly wrong. Last season I felt the SFA made too many demands with trips to places like Saudi Arabia and Malta. They must look more closely at the requirements of the clubs. In the World Cup run-up, though, Celtic will certainly try to be helpful by releasing players to prepare properly for internationals. I would never willingly pull a player out unless the reason was vital and genuine.

I'll probably never be the Scotland boss now and certainly not in the foreseeable future. I am back where I most want to be and have every intention of staying. If I'm fortunate enough to finish my career with Celtic I'll be one very happy and delighted man. Anyway, I see a trend to employ younger track-suited managers. I don't necessarily agree with this, but it's the directors who decide these things. I can only say I got myself into bother when I was young and aggressive and still learning my trade.

Looking at the international teams, I note that those who are successful usually have experienced managers. Having seen at close quarters in Spain and Mexico the pressures on World Cup bosses I feel this merely underlines the need for background, although younger people can assist. A manager who is tried and tested is what is necessary in international football.

I played under Ian McColl, Bobby Brown and Tommy Docherty. And The Doc for me was the best. John Prentice, in his short reign, didn't pick me and neither did Willie Ormond. Tommy had a different approach. He realised players were together for only a short time so everything had to be stimulating and exciting . . . and a lot of fun. I thought he was ideal for the Scotland manager's job.

If The Doc is with people too long he falls out with them. The short periods with the international players were ideal. I worked with him for three internationals. He chose me when I was 32 when other international managers had bombed me out. After the games with England, Northern Ireland and Wales there was a trip to Brazil. I discussed this with Jock Stein and he put me off. However, I wish now I had gone because it would have been nice to have experienced playing in such a great football country. The Doc even asked me to reconsider but I had gone ahead with holiday plans and these couldn't be changed.

I've always had the highest regard for The Doc. He brought me back into the international scene and I played well in the three games. I proved to a lot of people that I could still do well at this level. But The Doc disappeared soon afterwards to Manchester United. He then phoned and asked if I was interested in going to Old Trafford. I wasn't, so he bought big Jim Holton.

What I didn't enjoy about Tommy was that when I returned to Parkhead he gave me all sorts of advice in a newspaper column about players I should sign and criticised some of those that I had fixed up. He even had a buzz at the Celtic board for allowing me to go on a week's holiday before the season started. This annoyed and disappointed me. I don't feel, in any case, that he is in a position to tell me about Scots players because he rarely, if ever, sees them. However, I suppose that's Tommy!

As well as being a good international boss Tommy revitalised Manchester United which proved to me that he is a big team man, even when he keeps on stating that he has had more clubs than Jack Nicklaus.

Chapter Twelve

Games And Goals To Remember

THE DATE, 6 May 1970, is indelibly printed in my mind. After winning the League Cup and taking the League Championship from Rangers by a massive 12 points, Celtic failed to win the European Cup because of massive over-confidence and woeful misjudgment of the opposition in the most crucial game of the season. It was our second European Cup final and we were tipped so strongly to beat the Dutch team Feyenoord at the San Siro Stadium which, ironically, is the home of Inter Milan whom we defeated in the 1967 final.

We were on our nine-year run and it didn't matter which team we played against, we wanted to beat them. And usually did. On the run-up to the Feyenoord game we KO'd Basle of Switzerland, Benfica of Portugal, Fiorentina of Italy, and England's pride and joy, Leeds United. So nobody could say it was an easy passage to the final. In fact, there was a European record crowd of 136,505 at Hampden for the second semi-final with Leeds.

But let's go back a bit. Having eliminated Basle on a 2-0 aggregate in the first round, we met Benfica whose team included the great Eusebio. We won 3-0 at Celtic Park, and since we could easily have run up a much greater score it was hard to credit that any team would pull back such a lead against us. But, in Lisbon, just before half-time we lost two goals in four minutes when such a thing didn't even seem on the cards. Eusebio, who did so little in Glasgow that he was subbed to let them employ a defensive plan in the second half, hit an unsaveable shot and another goal followed quickly. In the second half it was backs-to-the-wall stuff but

Diamentino, only a youngster then, headed in from a corner kick with the official clock showing two minutes' injury time had been played. We actually thought the referee had blown for the end of the match. So it went into extra-time and we managed to survive, which meant there had to be a toss of the coin to decide the outcome of a game we should never have been in danger of losing.

Some of us packed into the referee's room. It was an incredible scene. The referee said there had to be another toss-up to decide whose honour it would be. I called "heads" and was right. Next time he threw the coin in the air there was a scatter of people. It was literally just settling on the floor when I shouted "heads" again. We all jumped up and were off. If I had been wrong I don't know what the referee would have done. I said to Jock Stein: "How would you have reacted if it had come down tails?"

His reply was straight to the point: "I would have kicked the coin before it even stopped rolling!"

Sean Fallon was out the door in a flash but Paul Wilson got in front of him and told the lads we had won before I was halfway back to the dressing-room. It is an astonishing way to decide an important game. I was sorry — honestly! — for Benfica who had fought back from a 3-0 defeat away from home. I remember that in the first match in Glasgow we got a free-kick in the second minute. We were wondering what to do but Tommy Gemmell told Bertie Auld: "Just touch it to me and I'll do the rest!" He hammered it into the net. Willie Wallace got a second four minutes from half-time and Harry Hood added another in the second half.

Benfica were one of the acknowledged greats at the time so it was a superb result. But these are the kind of games clubs have to live through in Europe. Victories are fought out, not because of planning or tactics, but by grit and endurance. We couldn't take much credit out of the fact that we reached the third round thanks to a lucky coin-toss, but the matches with Benfica still demonstrated what's important. Before we met Leeds we had to beat Fiorentina. A 3-0 lead from the first leg meant that a 1-0 defeat in Florence didn't matter.

It never failed to impress me at that time how Celtic produced quality players. Jim Brogan had pushed himself into the team as achievements continued. Obviously, over ten years personnel had to change and others who came in were Davie Hay, Lou Macari,

George Connelly, Danny McGrain and Victor Davidson, with Harry Hood moving to us from Clyde.

The contrast between the Milan final and our success in Lisbon was marked. But, like it or lump it, we didn't notice the difference between being underdogs and hot favourites. In fact, we thought we had more or less clinched it when we beat Leeds. They were hailed as the greatest team in Britain.

Our two games with Leeds were unforgettable. Jock Stein was very positive. The style in English football was to let the other team get the ball, then break up the attack after the midfield men had started to distribute it. Big Jock decided we weren't going to involve ourselves in this and we wouldn't under any circumstances be second best. Johnny Giles and Billy Bremner were very important. We put players on top of them and didn't give them an inch of room. It was very like the football Celtic played in the 1987-88 season. We pressured them constantly. George Connelly scored in the first minute and we had another goal disallowed in the second half. We won 1-0 but 3-0 or 4-0 would have been a fairer reflection of the play.

Big Jack Charlton was renowned for scoring goals and it was my responsibility to make sure he didn't get in any telling headers — which he didn't. Incidentally, Evan Williams had replaced Ronnie Simpson, who retired after the Cup final that year to end a career which went back to 3 June 1945, when he first played for Queen's Park. Naturally, I was sorry to see Ronnie go, but Evan was a better keeper than many thought.

At Elland Road, Jimmy Johnstone had one of the magical games that only he could produce. He beat four and five defenders at a time and ripped Terry Cooper apart. I doubt if any top-class left-back has ever had such a going-over. Wee Jimmy was simply marvellous. Big Jock changed things and used players such as Davie Hay while John Hughes subbed for Connelly and did extremely well.

Willie Wallace was left out of the second leg at Hampden but Hughes was in from the kick-off. That second game was astounding and the only time I felt worried was when, just after half-time, John Hughes levelled a goal by Billy Bremner. The atmosphere was fantastic. Running through my mind was the thought that if Leeds scored at 1-1 we were in trouble because of

Jock Stein, master tactician, preaches to the converted as we prepare again for Europe.

the rule that an away goal counts as two in a tie. However, I wasn't troubled for long. Bobby Murdoch thundered in a second goal four minutes later.

It had, in fact been touch and go whether I played. In the Scottish Cup final four days before I had injured an ankle but had to stay on for the entire game. I had only those four days to recover and didn't think I would be able to play against Leeds. The situation underlined the good sense of later introducing the use of substitutes. Had there been a stand-by on the bench I could have come off. As it was, I might have jeopordised everything by having to stay on against Aberdeen when I wasn't fit to do so. But it was a final and I couldn't leave it to ten mates. My daughter Paula was being christened the day after the Aberdeen game and I turned up wearing a slipper on my badly swollen foot. Nobody who saw me

I jump above Frank Munro as he comes forward for a corner kick in the 1967 Scottish Cup final against Aberdeen.

could have imagined I would play on the Wednesday in a European Cup semi-final. The unfortunate thing was that we had only one League game left after the semi before we played Feyenoord and there was no way I could be fit for a run out in it. However, since the 3-1 aggregate victory resulted in Celtic being called "Champions of Britain" it is worthwhile giving the teams:

At Leeds — *Leeds United:* Sprake, Reaney, Cooper, Bremner (Bates), Charlton, Madeley, Lorimer, Clarke, Jones, Giles, Gray. *Celtic:* Williams, Hay, Gemmell, Murdoch, McNeill, Brogan, Johnstone, Connelly, (Hughes), Wallace, Lennox, Auld.

At Hampden: — *Celtic:* Williams, Hay, Gemmell, Murdoch, McNeill, Brogan, Johnstone, Connelly, Hughes, Auld, Lennox. *Leeds United:* Sprake, (Harvey), Madeley, Cooper, Bremner, Charlton, Hunter, Lorimer, Clarke, Jones, Giles, Gray.

So much has been said about the reasons for us losing to Feyenoord that I think it must be made clear that we all shared in the glory of Lisbon so we had to accept that we were all a part of the defeat in Milan. To a man, we completely underestimated Feyenoord.

Jock Stein and Sean Fallon also misread the Dutch champions in their assessment of their strengths and weaknesses. Over-confidence was our undoing. Jock Stein compared them to St Johnstone, and by this he meant they were some way off the best. Saints finished 13th in an 18-club League and earlier in that season we had beaten them 1-0 in the League Cup final.

So we thought we were playing a middle-of-the-road team. In addition, because our season was ending, we didn't have games to play in our limber-up. Big Jock had been reluctant to hold special matches in case players were injured. So half of the team played in a charity match at Fraserburgh and the rest went to Gateshead before we left for Milan. We had only had one game together in the preparation period, and that was against Stenhousemuir at Celtic Park. There was no doubt our heads were full of broken bottles.

Some of the names had changed but we were still very close and proud to play for Celtic. The over-confidence, though, was close to a swagger. We stayed well out of the city at Varese and didn't like it. We had been there before and were not pleased to go back. We were so sure of winning that when Jock Stein read out the team he told George Connelly he was being left out at the start, although he had played well in the semi-finals. "You have plenty of time to be in another winning European Cup final," George was told, "but for some of the other lads this will be the last chance."

Willie Wallace came back in to the team. Don't get me wrong. Willie was always one of my favourites. But was it right to drop George although he did come on as a sub? A lot was made, too, about the players forming a "perks" pool and, indeed, a meeting was called on the morning of the game. It was claimed that this was the idea of the players. I can say categorically that this was not the case. Big Jock invited an agent — Ian Peebles — to Parkhead and told us that he would work for the pool and try to get us a few quid. It was definitely not the players who organised it.

I have to admit candidly that I contributed to the defeat because of a silly, impulsive action. But it was uncanny how everything went wrong. We scored after 30 minutes. Tommy Gemmell got the goal and over the years it's amazing the number he scored as a full-back which were so vital to Celtic. But after only two minutes Israel equalised and we had to hold on grimly to go into extra time.

We took the game into extra time at 1-1. Then I committed a remarkable crime — I handled the ball deep in the penalty area. I still can't understand why I did it. I had never been guilty of this before. I remember clearly the act of handling but the rest is hazy. Anyway, Kindvall swept past me to lob the ball into the net in 116 minutes. The referee, Concetto Lo Bello, of Italy, ignored the penalty possibility, giving the Dutch the advantage, so the goal stood. It was a correct decision but I'll never know if Kindvall would have scored if I hadn't stuck out my hand.

However, Feyenoord were a far better side than we were led to believe. Dutch journalists said immediately after the final whistle that we had misjudged their side. Scots are like that. We climb mountains, but when we get to the top we want to jump off. Losing to Feyenoord was a huge disappointment, but I assure you money was not what we worried about before, during or after the match. That has never been my style nor was it the way of any of my team-mates.

Here were the teams, although my mates won't thank me for the reminder — *Celtic:* Williams, Hay, Gemmell, Murdoch, McNeill, Brogan, Johnstone, Lennox, Wallace, Auld, (Connelly), Hughes. *Feyenoord:* Pieters Graafland, Romeyn, (Haak), Laseroms,

Israel, Van Duivenbode, Hasil, Jansen, Van Hanegem, Wery, Kindvall, Moulin.

Immediately after our flop the *Sunday Mirror* carried a story that Big Jock was pointing the finger at the players' pool and saying we had been more interested in making money than winning the trophy. This riled us because it simply wasn't true. I trace a decline in the relationship between Big Jock and the players directly to this. Oh, yes, we won things afterwards but we never got on as well again. Celtic went to America to play some games and the Big Man returned to Scotland early. In fact, so did Bertie Auld and Tommy Gemmell who were sent home after the Big Man had gone. I thought it regrettable that the club took such a step.

Undoubtedly, everyone admired Big Jock and respected his ability, but even the best make mistakes and he certainly made one by underestimating Feyenoord. He took his share of the glory in Lisbon — and was fully entitled to do so — but he shied clear of joining us in accepting the blame for defeat in Milan. A lot of it was double-Dutch to me as I spent the bulk of my time getting fit for the final and had to work very hard to do it.

The consolation of that Feyenoord final was that we had done so much, and enjoyed playing so tremendously, in our great championship run that we had plenty of memories to fall back on. Happy ones, that is. It astonishes me even now that 1970 was considered a disappointment on the strength of one game. As I've already pointed out, we were champions and League Cup-winners, not to mention being beaten Scottish Cup finalists — these were not bad achievements by any standards.

Celtic's fabulous run began on 24 April 1965. Jock Stein had returned to the club from Dunfermline in January and we went on in such a short time to win the Scottish Cup in a dramatic game in which I headed the winner — ironically, against the Fifers. It was the first time Celtic had won the Cup for 11 years and it had been Big Jock who last accepted the trophy as captain.

In our super victory over the Fifers we twice fell behind. Dunfermline scored their second to lead 2-1 two minutes from half-time. Bertie Auld scored twice. The first was following a shot by Charlie Gallagher which came off the bar. Bertie headed it in. I got the winner with nine minutes to go. Gallagher took the corner from the left. Charlie was a good striker of the ball. It was important that I timed the run properly — and I did. I got in front of everybody and headed into the middle of the net. Alex Smith, a good player, was detailed to frustrate me at corners and this was the first time I had had a clear run at the ball.

After the game we went to the Central Hotel in Glasgow for the after-match celebrations. We drove through Govanhill and what was the Gorbals in those days and it was pandemonium all the way. The fans were running on to the road in their excitement, trying to stop the bus. Motor cycle cops tried to guide us away from the supporters by switching the route. The scenes outside the hotel were fantastic. We had to go to a corner window to hold up the Cup and let the fans have a good look at it.

The euphoria was fantastic and, difficult though it may be to understand, supporters were different in those days. They didn't wear colours as obviously as they do now and, indeed, were a much more seriously dressed lot. It was a great game for me and also for Bertie Auld, who had returned to the club from Birmingham: here he was, snatching a couple of goals on such an important occasion. Of all the pictures we've had taken after special games, that's the one — the team and the scenes afterwards — which is in the manager's office. Big Jock began that tradition and I've kept it going. However, I'll make sure the 1988 team who won the League and Cup double also figure prominently on my office wall. I hope that we will make the same progress as we did after that 1965 victory. Until then I hadn't known what success was like although I had been a losing Scottish Cup finalist twice — against Rangers and Dunfermline.

I had made my debut in the first team on 23 August 1958, in a League Cup-tie against Clyde as stand-in for Bobby Evans who was injured. So it was seven years on before I got my hands on a major trophy. I had just missed a game all Celtic fans like to recall — on 19 October 1957 — when we beat Rangers 7-1 in the League Cup final at Hampden and Billy McPhail scored a hat-trick.

So, all of a sudden, things changed for Celtic with Big Jock at the helm. He had had success at Dunfermline and had put Hibs on the right lines before rejoining us. That final was the event which triggered everything off and it also gave an indication of the way fortunes were to change in Scottish football. Dunfermline were a really good side and they are still the team with the greatest potential who are not in the Premier League.

Apart from transforming Celtic from losers to winners, scoring the clincher made it especially memorable for me. Centre-halves don't have this kind of good fortune too often, although looking back I scored quite a few important goals.

In our 1967 European Cup-winning run I headed the winner against Vojvodina with 20 seconds to go at Parkhead when it seemed certain that we would have to play-off against the Yugoslavs in Rotterdam. Charlie Gallagher was again the guy who made the cross from a corner and once more I timed my jump to send the ball well out of the reach of their 'keeper. This put us into the semi-final against Dukla Prague.

In the infamous World Club Championship games with Racing Club I headed the winner at Hampden — again from a corner, though this time John Hughes sent the ball over. It sailed into the far corner of the net.

In the 1972 Scottish Cup final in which we beat Hibs 6-1, I snatched an early goal. In the second minute I lashed the ball in off Tom Callaghan's free-kick.

Three years earlier, when we beat Rangers 4-0 in the Scottish Cup final — with 132,870 watching! — I scored another second-minute goal in a really tough final which was the Ibrox club's first final defeat for 40 years.

I was lucky that the goals I scored were so important. If the ball was played in properly I usually had a good chance of getting to it.

Celtic-Rangers matches inevitably baffle the forecasters. Form means not a jot. The 1971 Scottish Cup final was a prime example. Aberdeen were our main challengers when we won the championship. They were only two points behind but Rangers were in fourth place trailing 15 points. Yet in the final Derek Johnstone was brought on to replace Andy Penman in the last 20 minutes and headed a fairytale equaliser — Bobby Lennox had scored five minutes from the interval — with just three minutes to go. Rangers knocked us out of our stride by their sheer determination. In the replay — with 103,332 looking on, 17,000 down on the first tie — we went 2-0 up in a 60-second burst starting with the 24th minute Lou Macari goal and followed by a Harry Hood penalty. Jim Craig got an own goal to make it 2-1. Willie Johnston patted Jim on the head and he didn't like it at all. It was important for us to win

My last gasp header finally ended Vojvodina's challenge. (D C Thomson).

Celtic line up for the European Cup final. Lisbon 1967.

because we had been such firm favourites and had seen a clear-cut victory snatched away by big "DJ".

The World Club Championship games with Racing Club of Buenos Aires were the most fantastic ever seen. Here we were in a state of high excitement about playing on another Continent. It was the Great Unknown. Penarol had come to Celtic Park for a game to mark the opening of our floodlights. They were magnificent. We beat them convincingly but, nevertheless, they were a team to be admired. This was a sample of South American football and we assumed Racing would be similar. What we hadn't realised was that Racing's tactician was the notorious Juan Carlos Lorenzo, who managed Argentina in the 1966 World Cup finals in England and whom we were to run up against seven years later as boss of Atletico Madrid. However, we quickly saw in the first match at Parkhead that Racing didn't particularly care how they defended so long as they didn't concede a goal. They sought a draw in Glasgow and didn't get it because of a well-placed John Hughes corner which I headed home. There was a lot of body-checking and general fouling. Coming off the pitch, the big defender Basile was waving and shouting about what would happen to us in Buenos Aires. I wondered how they behaved at home when it was necessary to score goals. I was to find out with a vengeance.

When we arrived in Buenos Aires, Argentina's capital, we were taken to a Country Club which I can only say contrasted sharply with the style Racing had been treated to in Scotland at the Marine Hotel in Troon. We were in rooms that were third-class, the servants' quarters, we thought at first. They made everything awkward for us. We had an interpreter who had a Scots background, and we found out later he was telling the Argentinians everything we were saying and doing. He was a spy in our camp rather than a helper.

We lost 2-1 but, had the present rules existed, we would have won on the away goal counting double. I remember we went on to the pitch carrying the Argentina flag, but instead of being pleased the fans took exception and all kinds of missiles began flying. Ronnie Simpson was hit by a piece of metal and, with blood streaming from a cut, it was clear he couldn't play. John Fallon replaced him. This is one of the advantages of having two good goalies on the staff.

We were robbed. There's no doubt in my mind about that. The first goal was so far offside it was frightening. I later saw pictures and it was a blatant blunder — or was it? — by a Uruguayan referee. Tommy Gemmell had earlier scored from a penalty which the ref had to give, but Jimmy Johnstone also had a goal knocked off when he doubled round the 'keeper. Incidentally, Tommy has the fantastic record of scoring in a World Club Championship and two European Cup finals. This is a ready-made question for a quiz night but it is also an exceptional fact. Anyway the match-handling and the behaviour of the fans were horrific. Racing went 2-1 ahead three minutes after the interval and that's the way it stayed.

Next there was a suggestion that Celtic shouldn't cross the River Plate to Montevideo for a play-off as a protest about the treatment which had been meted out. But not to go would have been a walk-out and Celtic were not prepared to condone this. We should have known what lay ahead when we arrived in Uruguay because the President had just asked for a day off — to fight a duel!

The game at the Centenario Stadium was an unbelievable disaster. The ground was ringed with barbed wire and there was also a six-foot moat running round the perimeter. The police were in riot gear and carried guns, long truncheons and tear-gas canisters. They used all of them during the game and were twice called on to the pitch by the paunchy Paraguayan referee, Rudolfo

Osorio, to restore order.

Our patience had snapped and we were in no mood to be mucked about. The first two players to go were Basile, who had done so much threatening at Parkhead, and Bobby Lennox. Imagine Wee Bobby being sent off! We thought it was a case of mistaken identity. He had spent 90 minutes in Buenos Aires being kicked all over the place along with Jimmy Johnstone and had barely protested. Jimmy and Bobby had obviously been picked out as danger men and off they went at the first opportunity. Unfortunately, the Penarol team who had played in Glasgow chatted to us before the game and they said the only way to treat Argentinian players was to kick them. So they had us all fired up. We were ready for anything.

It's an amazing thing about South Americans — excluding Brazilians — that they can be such delightful people, but at the drop of a hat they can change into something quite different. For a nation that is so athletic and with such fine players — World Cup winners in 1978 — Argentinians lapse into the role of assassins very easily and quickly. Racing won the World Club Championship because they set out to provoke. They wanted us to lose our cool and won because we did. We let ourselves down by falling right into the trap.

The Big Man was convinced the referee in Buenos Aires was biased. He said the name of the official was supposed to be drawn from a panel of three. The Argentinians said this was true but out came the name — Marinho, of Uruguay — which they had given us 24 hours before. The pitch in Montevideo was also bone dry and there was almost a path right down the middle. All in all, the bad omens were there from the start.

Eventually, so many players were sent off it was a joke. Bobby Lennox, Jimmy Johnstone and John Hughes all got their marching orders. So did Bertie Auld, though he refused to go. In the first incident in the most bizarre game in which I've ever played Jimmy Johnstone was hacked down by a brute called Rulli. We protested and, when the referee appeared to point to the pavilion, the Racing players went off their rockers. So police had to be called in. When everything quietened the referee ordered off not Rulli but Basile and Lennox.

Then, just after half-time Jimmy Johnstone was held by the

178

Racing skipper Martin and used his arms to get free. Martin ham-acted his way to the ground and lay there as if mortally wounded. So the Wee Man had to go and became the first Scot to be sent off abroad while under domestic suspension at home. Jimmy had had a 21-day ban slapped on him by the SFA but they had split it so that he could play in the World Club Championship.

The goalie Cejas was extraordinary. When anything happened he was in there punching and shoving. It became so bad that John Hughes walloped him and that's when he got his marching orders.

In the second half Bertie Auld committed an offence. The referee said: "Off". Bertie said he wasn't going. "Off, I tell you," said the ref imperiously.

Bertie replied: "I told you, I'm not going off."

The referee insisted that he was in charge but Bertie said he didn't care and implied that there wasn't much evidence of this, anyway. So, finally, the referee said he could stay on, and in a newspaper interview weeks later he confirmed that Auld had refused to be sent off — and he had agreed! It is the first and last time that a player at this level in football has been able to negotiate in such a way.

We were never quite sure about the insults hurled at us. They called us "animals" which was in revenge for what Sir Alf Ramsey had dubbed Argentina when they had played England in the 1966 World Cup and their player Rattin was sent off. They also compared us with the English in very voluble terms. We were made to suffer for their Wembley agonies.

I honestly felt we were a better team than Racing Club, but we lost our heads faced with provocation and rank bad refereeing. When a team is upset to the degree that we were it was hopeless. Rough play wasn't our scene anyway. We were robbed in the second game and, if we had disregarded the provocation and played nor-mally, we would have won in Montevideo. We lost a goal in 55 min-utes scored by Cardenas but it was a horrible game because, in addition to the five who went off, police were twice called to restore order. The police even went to the Press Box to ask Scottish journalists if they were pleased with the way the police had behaved as they were using water cannons on a section of the crowd.

Being the best in the world was an accolade I felt our team deserved. Instead, we came home to be fined £500 each by Celtic

— a lot of money in those days. So far as I have been able to establish no action was ever taken against Racing Club players. I thought it was harsh treatment for us in all the circumstances.

Another infamous collision with Latin temperaments involved our European Cup semi-final in 1974 against Atletico Madrid. This was supposed to be a quality match between two of the leading clubs. It was also my chance to reach a third final at a comparatively late stage in my career. In fact, Jimmy Johnstone, Bobby Lennox and myself were the only survivors from Lisbon still operating in the Celtic top team.

What a travesty the tie turned out to be. Atletico were managed by that man Juan Carlos Lorenzo, and he came to Glasgow with a team determined to draw. They had three players ordered off by a Turkish referee, Dogan Babacan, and seven booked. Remarkably, the ref didn't take out his black book once. He worked entirely by memory. Perhaps he was frightened about what might happen if he dared to look down even for a few seconds to write a name. We should have capitalised on our superiority at Parkhead but were too hasty and anxious to make our numerical advantage count. The play of the Spanish club was a disgrace and their treatment of Celtic, especially Jimmy Johnstone, was preposterous.

We went to Madrid under all kinds of pressure. There were discussions about not travelling but this could have meant a ban from Europe for Celtic and nobody wanted to risk that. The Latin nations, it seems to me, have a big say in the destiny of European football within UEFA, the governing body. I am never sure that British clubs get a fair crack of the whip. Certainly, after the first match UEFA should have done more than fine Atletico £14,000, warn them about their future conduct, and ban six players from the second leg. Any team who behaved as they did at Parkhead must have felt very fortunate not to be expelled from the competition.

When we arrived in Madrid the situation had been thoroughly dramatised. There was a threat that Jimmy Johnstone was to be shot, which didn't exactly delight the Wee Man. Big Jock thought the letter was the work of a crank but we couldn't take chances. Our hotel was surrounded by armed guards, which seemed designed to intimidate us as well as afford protection. When we arrived for the game and went out for the pre-match warm-up there was an awful row. They objected to us being on the field which was to say the least, unusual. The enmity which had been built up was terrible and Atletico switched the whole situation round to convince the Spaniards that they had been brutalised in Glasgow. Their fans were going potty when we ran out.

The thugs finally managed to score in 77 minutes when we were tiring. Garate tapped the ball in from a few yards and then we were caught going forward when we had dropped all caution to try to equalise. Adelardo hit a shot high into the net. Atletico didn't need to adopt hooligan tactics. They had some very good players. Lúis, who was getting a bit older, had class and there were several others around him. Why a team with so much quality should play in this way is not really a mystery. I put it down to their manager. It demonstrated the influence a team boss can have. I tend to the view that teams epitomise the personality of the manager. And Juan Carlos Lorenzo is somebody I will never invite home for dinner.

This tie produced another example of the split personality of Latins and it is too easy to say it is caused by different interpretations of the laws. The viciousness of Atletico was obvious and there was a strong Argentinian influence. The game should have been a showpiece and I wonder about the lead that youngsters get from games like this. The wrong things may have rubbed off. Football should be highlighted for its good aspects but they must be on display in the first place. I believe top players should be more mindful of the effect their actions can have on youngsters and particularly now that so many see games around the world on TV.

The teams for the two games were:

At Parkhead — *Celtic*: Connaghan, Hay, Brogan, Murray, McNeill, McCluskey, Johnstone, Hood, Deans (Wilson), Callaghan, Dalglish.

Atletico Madrid: Reina, Melo, Diaz, Benegas, Overjero, Eusebio, Ayala, Adelardo, Garate (Quique), Irueta (Albert), Heredia.

At Madrid — *Atletico*: Reina, Benegas, Capon, Adelardo, Heredia, Eusebio, Ufarte, Luis, Garate, Irureta, Becerra.

Celtic: Connaghan, McGrain, Brogan, Hay, McNeill, McCluskey, Johnstone, Murray, Dalglish, Hood, Lennox.

One thing did cheer us. In the final in Brussels Atletico were beaten 4-0 by Bayern Munich after a 1-1 draw.

Chapter Thirteen

Why "King" Kenny is such a Marvel

KENNY DALGLISH took over as player-manager of Liverpool at a terrible period in the club's distinguished history, immediately following the Heysel Stadium disaster in Brussels on 29 May 1985. All the managerial traps seemed to have been set for him: pitchforked from the dressing-room to boss team-mates who had just lost a European Cup under the shadow of a tragedy of 39 deaths and 400 injured which rendered the football irrelevant.

Dalglish succeeded me as the Celtic skipper in 1975 and is another and important Celtic influence on the British game. I feel that is good because we were schooled in attacking football — just as youngsters continue to be at Parkhead.

Kenny is a unique character but the thing which impresses me most about him is his single-mindedness. He has always done things his way. Many were surprised when, on taking over as manager, he axed Phil Neal and Alan Kennedy and spent £350,000 on Steve McMahon. That was the first sign to Liverpool people how determined Kenny can be. And how he is prepared to back his judgment. His single-mindedness, almost stubbornness, has helped him to go to the top and stay there. He has always been a hard trainer and wanted to come back and work overtime on his own if it was necessary. He has carried this through his football career. It's not luck which has made Kenny. He has the gift of natural talent but he had the determination, the ambition and the appetite always to try to do well.

I recall him as a youngster at Parkhead, not yet in the first team, but training with us in preparation for the start of the season. There was no doubt whatever that here was a tremendous talent for the future. Lou Macari has been quoted as saying that he didn't think Kenny was outstanding as a boy and that he had to work hard to develop himself. I couldn't disagree more. My very first look at him convinced me that Kenny would be a big name in football in the not-too-distant future. It was inevitable he was going to be one of the greats. I'm not saying we expected him to be the complete player that he turned out to be, but his ability just couldn't be disguised.

I tried to dissuade Kenny from going to England. I had stopped playing and was thinking as a Celtic supporter. Kenny felt he had fulfilled his ambitions at Parkhead and that it was time for him to move on and take up a new challenge. He had won everything except a European Cup medal. At that time he was almost carrying Celtic on his back so it was disappointing to see him go.

In 1977 I went to Rome to see Liverpool winning the European Cup 3-1 against Borussia Münchengladbach. Liverpool knew then that Kevin Keegan was moving to Hamburg and they told me: "We'll be taking Dalglish from Celtic." I said they had no chance. That was in May. Three months later Kenny was at Anfield. What an impact he made in England from the start. He took Liverpool by storm and he's done the same as a manager. Liverpool supporters quickly forgot about Kevin Keegan and wiping such a fine player from memory was a feat in itself.

Kenny has done everything essentially his way but a bit of praise, too, for the Anfield club. They have appointed managers from within since the days of the great Bill Shankly and have a streamlined organisation which others clubs have tried to emulate without much success.

The Dalglish record includes playing 102 times for Scotland. How did he achieve this coupled with his remarkable club performances? The outstanding aspect of his style was that he was the complete team player. He fitted into any pattern. Kenny wasn't like Jimmy Johnstone or George Best who were supreme individualists on the pitch. He harnessed a team and tied everything together. He made players round about him look better than they actually were. He is certainly the most accomplished player I ever played with. By far. He had magnificent skills but it was his ability as an all-rounder which made him so exceptional.

His career touched such heights at Anfield that Liverpool's chairman John Smith called him "the best player this club has signed this century". He cost a mere £440,000 and Bob Paisley had no doubt he was his bargain signing. Kenny has always had a dislike of the treatment table and in his first three years at Anfield he played 177 consecutive first-team matches. At the end of his first season he scored the winner in the European Cup final against FC Bruges at Wembley. These were the new horizons Kenny hankered after when he left Celtic.

League titles and Cup successes followed Kenny as though he was magnetic until he was appointed manager while still a very influential player. In fact, in his first season as the boss — 1985-86 — Kenny scored the goal against Chelsea which clinched the championship. Seven days later he was in the team which beat Everton in the FA Cup final. He became the first player-manager to win the double.

Season 1986-87 ended with Liverpool trophy-less and instant critics speculated that the party might be over for Liverpool. This was nonsense. Dalglish's single-mindedness brought a quick adjustment and in season 1987-88 Liverpool won the League title in a runaway performance though they lost 1-0 to Wimbledon in an FA Cup final which they were expected to win easily. Faced with the loss of Ian Rush to Juventus — he returned to Anfield in August after only a year in Italy — Kenny had bought John Barnes from Watford and Peter Beardsley from Liverpool. It was entrepreneurial genius but Dalglish was driven to spend by the sheer practicalities of team-balancing based on his own assessments backed up by that of the Liverpool machine. I had hoped last season that we would both complete the double on the same day but fate decreed otherwise. However, winning the First Division title in England is an awesome feat so Liverpool didn't complain despite their Wembley disappointment.

I would like to see more ex-Celts in charge of clubs. It would be good for the game. Celtic's approach is cavalier and none of us who have come through the Parkhead school — like "King" Kenny and myself — are ever likely to forget this. One thing I can't resist saying. Dalglish's signing for Celtic must have riled Rangers more than somewhat. He lived in high flats overlooking Ibrox and that's where his dad used to take him as a lad to watch games. Ah, well,

A youthful Kenny Dalglish boards the Celtic team bus in the company of Willie Wallace and Tommy Gemmell.

we can all make mistakes!

Scots fans and critics made blunders, too. In the early part of his international career Dalglish's right to be in the side was quite often challenged. The Hampden supporters could not see his value to the team, and it wasn't until he was on the high road to his first 50 caps that he was accepted as being vital to the Scotland set-up. Scots didn't recognise at first that here was a player so outstanding that, given his head, he would orchestrate everything. Undoubtedly, that's what Liverpool allowed him to do. He was, and still is, a winner.

Kenny is a reticent man. Because he didn't have "the gift of the gab" many suspected that he might not make a success of the PR side of his job. I have to admit I was among the doubters. For the first time I underestimated Kenny and the organisation which has been at Anfield for such a long time. Kenny stepped into the shoes of Bill Shankly, Bob Paisley and to a lesser extent Joe Fagan. They had set the standards. Shankly and Paisley particularly had a spectacular record of successes. It was not the act most of us would have chosen to follow. But Kenny has gone on to plot triumphs without worrying about any extra pressure which the pundits thought was on him because of past victory levels. Unhappily he cannot, at the moment, display his shrewdness at European level, but I hope the UEFA ban will not be an indefinite one.

I feel Kenny's single-mindedness kept him from encompassing too wide a circle for advice. Basically, he's done what he has considered to be right. And there can be nothing but the highest praise for what he has achieved at a ground where the fans have the highest requirements.

Always, of course, Jock Stein was the number one for me but I have never modelled myself on him or any other person. Carbon copies are not as good as the original, so it pays to do your own thing. The most unusual style of management came from Ally MacLeod whom I followed at Pittodrie. As I said earlier, Ally was heavily slammed after Argentina but I don't go along with the theory that he is a poor manager. He is one of the few who are not products or disciples of the SFA school of coaching at Largs. Others are myself and Graeme Souness. Surely the fact that Ally has taken Ayr United back to the First Division this season indicates he has ability. Ally, of course, does things much differently from me. He is an eccentric, but I like being in his company. It doesn't matter what he's talking about, he becomes so enthusiastic he makes it interesting. Wrapped up in all this is a deep and determined love of football. He brings a sparkle to it.

Willie Ormond was also somebody I admired — although he never picked me! He had a Bob Paisley approach. He was almost a father figure, a gentle man who liked a laugh. I always felt totally relaxed with him. The job he did with St Johnstone in the late Sixties and early Seventies was tremendous. He had them up there fighting with the top-dogs. His record with Scotland was excellent. He picked the players and let them get on with it. He usually chose

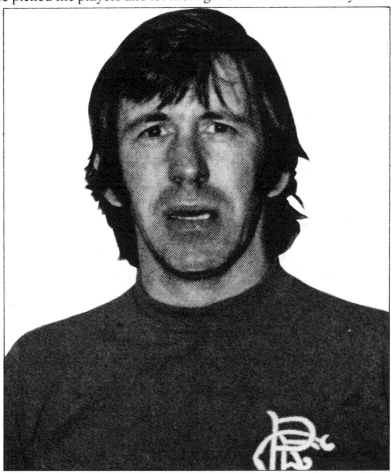

John Greig — a smashing contemporary.

the right men and at international level this is a special skill. He also had good understanding with the stars and particularly his captain, Billy Bremner.

John Greig was a smashing contemporary of mine both as player and manager. His attitude regarding Rangers was very similar to my own towards Celtic. He was wholeheartedly dedicated to making Rangers successful, so he was a man after my own heart — except, of course, that my loyalty was and is to a different club! I like him as a person, but the difficulty he had at Ibrox was stepping straight from being a player to management. Dalglish, of course, did it at Anfield but there are few people or personalities who could succeed by this route. Kenny had the advantage that he was still playing a leading part on the pitch and the players under his control must have respected his abilities. Greig, with no experience as manager, took over the hot seat at Ibrox when some of his playing pals were still in the side.

I had distanced myself by going to other clubs but, even when I returned to Celtic, I may have come back too quickly from Aberdeen. Still, I was away for a few years and this undoubtedly helped. In management decisions have to be made that are tough — and maybe on individuals. Sympathy is a fine thing, but let it interfere in football management and you're in trouble.

John Greig was unfortunate. The demand for success at both Parkhead and Ibrox is unrelenting. The pressure on a manager to provide trophies is overwhelming at times. I felt John got a raw deal from some sections of the media. He was almost pilloried at one stage. A radio phone-in programme seemed to be very nearly vindictive towards Greig as the Ibrox manager. I sympathised greatly with him.

Nowadays I feel it is imperative to have experience in football management to run a big club. It is important to work with other managers and smaller clubs. I realise in saying this that I could be misconstrued about Graeme Souness. But he may fall into the same category as Dalglish. Certainly, Rangers players could not fail to relate to his talents on the park even if he is now "rationing" his appearances. He was one of the most influential stars Scotland ever had. Liverpool got it right. They took him from Middlesbrough to supplement Dalglish and the two were the backbone for a long time. Bringing Souness to Ibrox was tremendously imaginative and has had a dramatic effect on the affairs of Scottish football.

Graeme is also in a position where he can compete with any club for whoever he wants to buy. Every manager would like to have this chance. Whether the others would be courageous enough to make the same decisions is something I don't know. The easiest thing in the world is to say: "Go and buy." But if you are the guy who has to stand or fall on a huge player investment it becomes another ball game.

I applaud Graeme as a rival manager for the things he has done although he is honest and admits he has made a mistake or two. Who hasn't? After getting everything right he found himself in the position of being the fastest gun. Everyone wanted to have a shot at him. That's the situation we are now facing and it is difficult. The players Souness bought are good. He was unfortunate to lose Terry Butcher because of injury last season but he may well make a big impression this season. Because a manager pays big money for a player it doesn't mean he will be a success. Brian Clough says it's easy to criticise managers who've spent a million or more pounds on a player who doesn't work out, but he added: "I can't slate them . . . because I've done it as well!"

Last season I thought Graeme had it right in Europe. They played really well against Dinamo Kiev, though later things fell apart. He really had two teams to pick as some of his signings couldn't play in Europe, being ineligible because of the date of joining at Ibrox. Possibly that weighed against him.

By the way, Graeme coming to Ibrox after playing all his senior football in England and Italy surely helps to knock the idea that a Scots manager can't succeed in the south or abroad. West Germans, Dutch, Danes, Yugoslavs . . . oh, a host of other countries, have managers and coaches working abroad, so why shouldn't Scots succeed too?

Alex Ferguson seems to be heading in the right direction with Manchester United though his job is difficult. United haven't won the English First Division Championship since 1967. It's astonishing, as they had money at their disposal to buy the best in the country. The demands on Alex are great, but United are the right vehicle for a manager with ability and, just wait, these forecasts of doom for Scots managers in England are about to be scotched. United can buy where and when they want and one example was their swoop for Brian McClair.

George Graham is the classic example of a fine player who went out and about to learn the business of coaching and management with lesser clubs. His last stop before going back to Highbury, where he performed so well as a player, was Millwall. He served his apprenticeship in the right way and I have liked George's approach since he took over at Arsenal. He has done everything his way and makes no bones about it. He has put his stamp on the club and has succeeded because of his own efforts. When directors hire a manager it is important to have confidence in him to make the decisions about buying and selling players — otherwise what is the point of having a team boss at all?

George, of course, is as Scottish as me, but has spent longer in England as player, coach and manager. But, like Kenny Dalglish, he has retained his accent and is still proud of the fact that he went to school in Bargeddie. That was what Bill Shankly said when Kenny first went to Anfield: "Don't over-eat . . . and don't lose your accent!" Good advice, I'd say.

Jim McLean at Dundee United . . . now there's a man who can be hard to understand but whose feats have been outstanding. He has hoisted the Tannadice club among the top teams and has moved them out of the mould of second-class citizens in direct opposition to one of the once big names in the game, Dundee. He has turned football on Tayside upside down. Before the advent of Jim McLean United were a bit like Partick Thistle — and, of course, I don't make the comparison unkindly.

He has performed wonders and I don't mean to diminish Jim's achievements by saying he has been given more time to get success than he would have been with the Old Firm. However, the manner in which he has developed United and kept them in the forefront ever since pinpoints his status as an outstanding manager. I doubt very much if anybody could have done more. His patience has been extraordinary. He was tempted to go to Rangers just before Jock Wallace returned for a second time. I would have been interested to see how Jim would have fared at Ibrox, The fact that he didn't take the job is the only question-mark on his outstanding career. He seemed hesitant about running such a big team. Jim has elevated United, possibly above their station, so I wonder why he didn't have the confidence to take over at Ibrox? At the time, I thought this would have been the very challenge he needed.

There certainly doesn't seem much left for him to achieve at Tannadice. In a way he has made life difficult for himself. Undoubtedly, he has taken United to a position where they are always expected to be in the running for honours. Getting to the UEFA Cup final, only to lose to the Swedish team Gothenburg over two legs (1-0 in Sweden and 1-1 in the return) was a great shame. Interestingly, United fans were awarded a FIFA trophy for their outstandingly good behaviour and Gothenburg were among those who made the recommendation. I had hoped, as much for Jim's benefit as for the club, that United would win a European trophy — and maybe they will yet! Jim McLean has proved his ability to coach and rear and develop his own talent. He has to be much respected for that.

As a person, Jim is unusual. He lives for football, and I wonder if he should find some other avenue for relaxation, although last year I have never seen him so laid-back. And he took United to the Scottish Cup final against us! What he has achieved is great and, though he may feel an overwhelming loyalty to the club, he has more than repaid anything they have done for him.

The fine of £4,000 imposed by the SFA last July with a three-year dug-out ban was horrific. Jim must have anticipated he would be disciplined over a half-time incident at Dens Park when United met Aberdeen in the Scottish Cup. But surely not as savagely. Managers feel there is an imbalance. There is no way in which they can properly register a protest. I have a lot of sympathy with Jim McLean although I face the fact that the lead we give must improve. Nobody at official level asks on a regular basis for our views. That's what is causing a great deal of frustration.

Two other managers — or should I say co-managers? — who have performed superbly for their club are Alex MacDonald and Sandy Jardine. They have formed a team which has been really successful and they have a respect for each other which makes their partnership work. It is tremendous for football that they have helped to turn Hearts around so efficiently.

Hearts are back as one of the country's most powerful teams and, between them, MacDonald and Jardine have brought the kind of determination to the club which means the players are tenacious and always refuse to surrender. They have worked steadily in their rebuilding of the team, and there can be few who don't admire the prudent way they have set about buying players within the resources of the club. Even in adversities like a goal-difference League Championship defeat by Celtic in the last game of season 1985-86 or a Cup semi-final defeat in the last couple of minutes against us at Hampden last season, they have kept things bubbling and never lost their ambition.

Both Alex and Sandy, of course, were good players themselves and, if I say that Alex was the more determined and dogged, it is merely to underline that this is the attitude he has taken with him into management. The way Hearts play reflects more of Alex's character then Sandy's, who was the more refined player. Hearts have the same bulldog-style attitude that Alex showed himself on the field. However, management teams cannot be duplicates. A contrast is essential and Sandy clearly makes an important contribution with his vast knowledge of the game at all levels. I feel sure this is also the opinion of chairman Wallace Mercer.

There is a lot of good management in Scottish football — at director level as well — and this is why there is a boom in the Scottish game.

Chapter Fourteen

My Élite Elevens

PICKING teams from the past is never easy so I will confine my choice to players who have been in the same side as me at some time. I hope friends whom I have left out will understand that I can name only eleven.

I have often thought about the best Celtic team of my time and, after careful deliberation, I have such a strong feeling for the Lisbon Lions that I simply can't see past them. My choice must be based on them although I will risk outrage and make three changes. I have to look at players who came later and judge if they would have improved the side. It's astonishing how few come into this category. In fact, I would bring in only Danny McGrain, George Connelly and Kenny Dalglish. This means leaving out Jim Craig, John Clark, and Steve Chalmers. Imagine having a team good enough to pass over this trio!

Danny McGrain is the best right-back I ever played with and there can also be no hesitation about bringing in Dalglish. George Connelly, instead of John Clark, is no reflection on the skill of the guy who played alongside me and was my assistant manager both at Aberdeen and Parkhead.

So now you ask the trick question: would my new-look team have beaten the Lions? Well, they might not have beaten them but it would certainly have been an improvement! Everything about picking old teams is hypothetical and, of course, not a little nostalgic. I've had to leave out Joe McBride who was as good a striker as anybody would want. Dalglish is ahead of him because of his fantastic all-round ability. There was also the pace of Bobby

One of the happiest moments of my life. This is me leading the team out, with Tommy Craig, to receive the Championship trophy.

Lennox and the sharpness of Willie Wallace. Paddy Crerand has to be overlooked, too, and he was a wonderful player. I also thought Harry Hood was especially good.

Here is a surprise. Brian McLaughlin was the most outstanding youngster I've ever seen. He came to Celtic as a lad in the early Seventies and made the same kind of impact as Dalglish on the senior players. He broke through to the top team quickly with two-footed passing ability. He was also a fair striker of the ball, with snappy pace and the ability to take people on. Unhappily, McLaughlin suffered a horrific knee injury against Motherwell and this effectively ended his career with Celtic. It was a tragedy for Brian, for Celtic and for football. I feel he would have been one of the all-time greats. It took Brian some time to get his confidence and determination back. He moved on to Ayr United and subsequently went to Motherwell. It was to Brian's eternal credit that he was still a good player, but the knee injury had taken away

194

some of his pace and sharpness. He still retained his shooting and passing ability but I felt sad because there's no doubt he would have been brilliant. He is the nearest I have seen to Scotland producing a Johan Cruyff type of player.

Explaining my changes in more depth, I feel Danny had that bit extra quality and class compared to Jim Craig whose big asset was the way he could break forward. Danny had more composure on the ball and would have edged Jim.

George Connelly was a unique player because he had stature and was a really great passer. The fact that he left the game so dramatically was really another tragedy for all concerned and particularly for the player himself. George would have been a truly great stalwart had he stayed in football. He had already proved himself at club and international level. He dislodges John Clark simply because of the magnitude of his all-round ability.

John Clark and I go back a long way. I arrived at Parkhead just ahead of him and we both come from Lanarkshire. We formed a close relationship despite the fact that we are different types of people. Whereas I am outgoing, John was quiet and almost introverted. He was the best read man on football I have known. He devoured the sports columns and football magazines and knew more about foreign teams than any of us because of this. When we retired from the playing side John became my assistant at Pittodrie and returned with me to Parkhead. We had a very good working partnership for a long time. Oddly enough, we never really mixed socially but on trips abroad as players we often shared a room. Our understanding broke up a little towards the end when John was linked with Partick Thistle and Kilmarnock. The newspaper reports came as a surprise on both occasions. However, it was interesting that two such different people could get on for such a long time on the pitch and then in management.

When Jim Brogan and Davie Hay played beside me, I also got on very well with them. But to improve the Lions — and I stress that word — Connelly would be the guy who would win my vote. I leave Davie Hay out with difficulty. He was a smashing ball-winner who had a lot of all-round ability and, had Danny not been around, he might have come in at full-back although he would have been more than useful in midfield. The team I have chosen is, of course, geared to the era. Davie's strength in midfield is something which

Two major Glasgow figures — Jack McGinn and the former Lord Provost at Glasgow — show the silverware.

would be needed in the modern-day game. I never played with Paul McStay or I might have been tempted to include him.

No explanation is needed about Kenny Dalglish. He was magnificent and I am sure Stevie Chalmers would agree. I've thought about others, such as Lou Macari, who might have come in but it's impossible to look past Kenny. If we could have had all these players together at the same time Celtic would have been unbeatable. That would have been Utopia.

The team I've selected would still do well in present-day football. They would have to adjust to other demands but I'm sure they would have done so. I don't think they would have to lose their individuality. I believe in this quality within a framework. They would have pleased the fans all right and that's paramount.

So, again with apologies to those who are left out, here is my Celtic élite eleven: Ronnie Simpson, Danny McGrain, Tommy Gemmell, Bobby Murdoch, Billy McNeill, George Connelly, Jimmy Johnstone, Willie Wallace, Kenny Dalglish, Bertie Auld and Bobby Lennox.

A Scotland team is difficult because of the number of good

players with whom I operated. As a goalkeeper Bill Brown, until the emergence of Jim Leighton, was out on his own in my book. He was magnificent and was a splendid team man. He had great command of his area. The full-backs would be Danny McGrain and Tommy Gemmell. Tommy might be a controversial choice but, in my opinion, he offered a lot to the game and he was always liable to score a goal.

I take the liberty of picking myself — which can always be done if you are the sole selector! — and I would like John Greig beside me. The other centre-halves of note in my time were Ian Ure, Ronnie MacKinnon and John Martis. Because of his strength, ability and wholehearted attitude Greig could have played in several positions. He played more than adequately at right-back, left-back and midfield. In fact, he scored a spectacular goal for Scotland coming from right-back against Italy in the last minute of a World Cup qualifying tie at Hampden in November 1965.

We have two good attacking full-backs in McGrain and Gemmell. It would be up to Greig and myself to provide the bulwark in the heart of the defence. I always enjoyed playing beside John.

My midfield would be Billy Bremner, Dave Mackay and Jim Baxter. I think these three would be good in any era. Bremner had undoubted ability and sharpness. He was a great international and club man as well as being a fine Scots skipper. Davie Mackay is one of the best players I ever saw. There was nothing he couldn't do on the park. He had personality, could shoot, pass and communicate well with the rest of the team. Jim Baxter was the most skilful midfielder Scotland has ever produced. Some said he could only perform when he was actually in possession. This was a view I couldn't understand. In his heyday Jim did a lot of work because of his uncanny judgment. This, of course, allowed him to be on the ball more than the others. And he could produce a special bit of genius which could transform a game.

Up front I am going for Jimmy Johnstone, Kenny Dalglish and Denis Law. Kenny and Denis played together towards the end of Law's career. But the younger Law and Dalglish would have been a magnificent pairing. Chuck in Jimmy Johnstone and we have a lot of players with flair.

So we have a back four capable of stabilising a game, a midfield who would win the ball and also be creative, which is something I always insist upon. If midfielders are just ball-winners they will also give it away whereas, if you have creative players, you're in control. Dalglish's flair, Johnstone's incredible talent and Law's striking power would make it a great front three.

I've had to leave out Bobby Murdoch and George Connelly which I don't like. But only eleven can go on the park at any one time. Also, I've passed over the late John White, of Spurs, who was dubbed "The White Ghost" because of the way he drifted around in games to surprise the opposition. He could have fitted into the midfield nicely. Another I considered good for Scotland was Davy Wilson. Although mainly right-footed, he played mostly on the left wing. He score a lot of goals and was a good all-rounder.

I feel this élite Scotland eleven would have been magnificent: Bill Brown (Spurs), Danny McGrain (Celtic), Tommy Gemmell (Celtic), Billy McNeill (Celtic), John Greig (Rangers), Billy Bremner (Leeds United), Dave Mackay (Spurs), Jim Baxter (Rangers), Jimmy Johnstone (Celtic), Kenny Dalglish (Liverpool) and Denis Law (Manchester United).

Chapter Fifteen

The Way Ahead for Celtic

IT IS amazing the pressure managers are under to sign expensive big-name players. Fans are obsessed with the idea of clubs spending money. This is one of the effects of Graeme Souness's plunge into the market in such a big way. It has been dramatic. Rangers provided the flame which ignited the Scottish scene. Everywhere I go now fans ask who my next big signing will be.

I do not accept that the way ahead for Celtic is to buy players one after the other. The main part of Celtic's team will consist of lads who have come through the ranks and have developed a feeling and understanding for the club. One thing which is essential in the future and which I felt, disappointingly, had stuttered a bit in the four years that I was away, was the reserve strength. It should have been better.

Celtic have still produced, or found, good young players like Anton Rogan, Derek Whyte and Peter Grant. If they join as youngsters it gives them a much greater depth of feeling for Celtic. Look at our team last season. One of the reasons we won the League and Scottish Cup double was that the players felt their responsibilities so profoundly. There was a tremendous atmosphere in the dressing-room and on the pitch. My belief is that this kind of feeling for the club and general enthusiasm is generated because players have signed as schoolboys and progressed through all the playing levels.

We'll have to work harder than we've ever done with the youngsters. Last season my attention was concentrated on the top team because of the job we had to do to get into a winning groove.

But I will be looking much harder at other aspects of the club — without minimising the importance of the top team — along with our chief scout John Kelman. He has a very important role. Interestingly, I wanted to take John to Aberdeen but he didn't fancy the idea. But he had no hesitation about joining Celtic because he is very much a fan of the club, This is what is essential and it is an attitude I intend to build on.

John is an expert talent-spotter. For example, he went over to Ireland and discovered Anton Rogan and Allen McKnight with Distillery. These signings certainly paid off. However much we may regard Ireland as a good hunting-ground for Celtic we've never been all that successful in recent years — Pat Bonner excepted, of course. So, under the noses of the leading English scouts, Kelman pulled out two players like this, which demonstrates his ability.

A chief scout's job is to develop connections which ensure that the right kind of raw talent is steered to Celtic. Our ability to promote and develop young talent must be improved. I've already taken steps in this direction and will be initiating other moves. John will keep me aware of the youngsters who show enough promise to be at Parkhead. Young talent will always be vital to us. We don't — as some other clubs do — sign boys willy-nilly and hope that we'll get something. We vet them and take lads we feel will progress all the way to the first team. We will not always be right, of course, because it's very difficult to judge positively.

I take the same care signing a youngster that I would with a big-money star. I don't want to waste my time, that of the coaches who will be working with them or, indeed, upset the feelings of youngsters unnecessarily by building them up and dropping them. Schoolboys we sign must look as though they might make our first team. I don't sign kids for the sake of keeping them away from other clubs. I try to be aware of who the lads are and, certainly, by the age of 16 when they're being called up I must know all about them. I don't want them to be names on a bit of paper.

Football is much more competitive than it has ever been. The 'S' form was a good thing for the Scottish game as it gave us the right to sign schoolboys and give them proper coaching. It went some way to prevent English clubs from poaching Scottish talent, but I still feel we don't do enough. The English clubs shouldn't really bid for

Me with the first team squad at Barrowfield, 1987.

The Celtic player pool and backroom staff for season 1988-89.
Back row: McGhee, Stark, Baillie, McCarthy, Rogan, Whyte.
Middle row: Physio Brian Scott, Traynor, Burns, Rough, Bonner, Andrews,
McAvennie, Archdeacon, Assistant Manager Tommy Craig.
Front row: Miller, Grant, Aitken, me, McStay, Morris, Walker.

our boys until they are school-leaving age, but it happens despite the rules. It is important to keep our developing talent at home. Senior players now have much greater freedom of movement but we should have the first chance to develop youngsters and see them coming into the Scottish game. I don't feel boys will get any better tuition in England.

I can never see Celtic as a chequebook-type club. I am not saying we will never dabble in the £1 million market but I would prefer not to do so. Last season we lost Brian McClair for £850,000, Mo Johnston for £375,000, Murdo MacLeod for £250,000, Alan McInally for £225,000, Paul McGugan for £70,000 and Mark Smith went to Dunfermline for £50,000. Basically, what I did was spend this money to build a championship side. But I would not expect the directors to provide me with an open chequebook. Nor do I want to sign players for the sake of it.

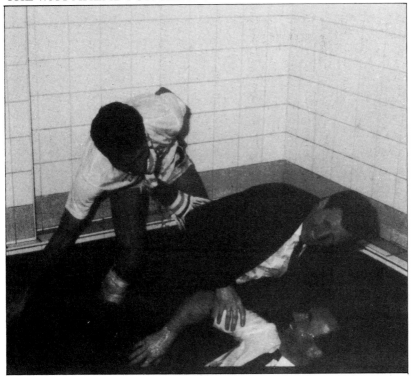

Bathed in success.

The introduction of freedom of contract was fair, and I think there should be an easy price scale based on a player's age and the wages he is being paid by a selling club. I cannot accept that a part-time club can pay a player £50 a week and expect to get £1 million. It's just not on. I also think all transfers should be conducted before the season starts and that no deals should be allowed in the playing season. Clubs should have to work with the same pool throughout. In my view this would be fairer although it would be a greater test of a manager's judgment.

A few years ago we looked at the Italian scene and wondered how players could move for such vast amounts of money. Now supply and demand has British clubs paying very nearly the same kind of sums. I worry about the rich becoming richer but what to do about it is another matter. I certainly don't think any club can be told to limit the cash they want to fork out on signings. If they think they can afford it then that's their business.

At Celtic Park we have faced up to the fact that we must bring in money from commercial ventures. The money at the gates no longer pays the bills. Fans say gates will go up 10,000 or 20,000 if you buy a new player, but in practice this doesn't happen. One thing which can be said about football is that it's been imaginative. And this has resulted in good schemes to generate cash. I still think the game is the most attractive spectator sport in the world. Yet I don't think we derive the advertising benefits of other sports such as motor-racing and tennis. Nigel Mansell talks of £4 million contracts in motor-racing but I don't see advertisers or sponsors getting the kind of return they could expect if they paid the same to a star footballer or a top team. Our game is the most natural sport for fans. Oddly, TV appears to have double standards. Certainly, other sports don't have the same advertising restrictions.

I am not in favour, by the way, of a Super League, because I am against élitism. Teams emerge and it is wrong to cut off their ambition. The game is about competition but, in truth, we're caught in a crossfire. If we don't raise the cash commercially to keep the good players, and improve on the quality we have, it could be a disaster.

Last season I was delighted to retain Paul McStay at Parkhead. There are players who can be allowed to move without any major effect, but there are others who are irreplaceable. Such a person is Paul McStay. Over the years if Celtic hadn't lost Dalglish, Macari, Hay, McClair and Johnston what a difference it would have made to the long-term development of the club.

Celtic have the chance now to make a firm base on which to conduct future operations. My intention is to create a system that will keep them powerful, not just in the short term, but long after my time. I want to help to provide a structure which will allow Celtic to hold on to the best players.

The most successful club in recent times is Liverpool. They've kept going without appointing a new manager from outside. They have set up a system and make it work continuously. That's what I want to do for Celtic. I'm not saying we'll mimic Liverpool. We'll devise a plan to suit our club. The importance of having a strong first team is not only to win matches in the Premier League. Such a squad will provide the breathing-space for youngsters to come through without being under pressure and hopefully a Nicholas, a

McStay or a Whyte will emerge. However, youngsters with less talent need more time and protection.

The slate is wiped clean in football every season. Kenny Dalglish won the double at Liverpool in his first season as manager and in the next his team didn't win anything. Liverpool didn't say that, because of this, the system was wrong. They continued doing the things they believed to be right. In the process they lost Ian Rush, the most consistent scorer in the country, but with the money they bought John Barnes and Peter Beardsley. It is significant that Liverpool are now stressing youth development and they have employed a Scot, Malcolm Cook, to supervise this. They recognise it isn't possible to go on and on buying stars.

Celtic are unusual among big clubs. People ask what the special Celtic feeling is all about and I can't answer specifically. It's something that grows on a player and adds an extra dimension. It is our twelfth man.

Appendix One

BILLY McNEILL — THE FACTS

BORN at Bellshill on 2 March 1940, and educated at Our Lady's High School, Motherwell.

First Celtic top-team game: 23 August 1958, League Cup, centre-half against Clyde at Parkhead. Celtic won 2-0.

Last match for Celtic: 3 May 1975, Scottish Cup final, centre half versus Airdrie at Hampden. Celtic won 3-1.

Played in 12 Scottish Cup finals, winning seven times, while in the League Cup he was successful on six of his nine appearances.

Total appearances for Celtic: 832.

First Briton to collect the European Cup: 25 May 1967 at Estadio Nacional, Lisbon. Captained the Celtic side which beat Inter Milan 2-1.

Awarded the MBE November 1974.

Appointed Clyde manager 1 April 1977. Moved to Aberdeen on 14 June of the same year.

Returned to Celtic Park on 28 May 1978. In the next five years led Celtic to three championship victories and also won the Scottish Cup and the League Cup once. They played 180 League matches winning 114, drawing 33 and losing 33.

Appointed manager of Manchester City on 2 July 1983, and after two years took them to the First Division as the third-placed promotion side.

Left for Aston Villa on 22 September 1986, and was sacked eight months later. Within a few days — on 28 May 1987 — Billy was re-appointed to manage Celtic. In the first season back he led them to the Premier League Championship and Scottish Cup double in Celtic's centenary year.

European Record

Season	Competition	Opposition	Scores (Celtic first)	Aggregate
1962-63	Fairs Cities Cup	Valencia	2-4 2-2*	4-6
1963-64	Cup Winners Cup	Basle	5-1 5-0	10-1
		Dinamo Zagreb	3-0 1-2	4-2
		Slovan Bratislava	1-0 1-0	2-0
		MTK Budapest	3-0 0-4	3-4
1964-65	Fairs Cities Cup	Leixoes	1-1* 3-0*	4-1
		Barcelona	1-3 0-0	1-3
1965-66	Cup Winners Cup	Go Ahead Deventer	6-0 1-0	7-0
		AGF Aarhus	1-0 2-0	3-0
		Dinamo Kiev	3-0* 1-1	4-1
		Liverpool	1-0 0-2	1-2
1966-67	European Cup	FC Zurich	2-0 3-0	5-0
		Nantes	3-1 3-1	6-2
		Vojvodina	0-1 2-0	2-1
		Dukla Prague	3-1 0-0	3-1
		Inter Milan	2-1 (Final)	
1967-68	European Cup	Dinamo Kiev	1-2 1-1	2-3
1968-69	European Cup	St Etienne	0-2 4-0	4-2
		Red Star	5-1 1-1	6-2
		AC Milan	0-0 0-1	0-1
1969-70	European Cup	Basle	0-0 2-0	2-0
		Benfica	3-0 0-3	3-3
			(Celtic won on toss of a coin)	
		Fiorentina	3-0 0-1	3-1
		Leeds United	1-0 2-1	3-1
		Feyenoord	1-2	
			(Final after extra time)	
1970-71	European Cup	Kokkda	9-0 5-0	14-0
		Waterford	7-0 3-2	10-2
		Ajax	0-3 1-0	1-3
1971-72	European Cup	BK 1903 Copenhagen	1-2 3-0	4-2
		Sliema Wanderers	5-0 2-1	7-1
		Ujpest Dosza	2-1 1-1	3-1
		Inter Milan	0-0 0-0	
		(Semi-final, Inter won 5-4 in penalty shoot-out at Parkhead after extra-time.)		
1972-73	European Cup	Rosenburg	2-1 3-1	5-2
		Ujpest Dosza	2-1 0-3	2-4
1973-74	European Cup	TPS Turku	6-1 3-0	9-1
		Vejle	0-0* 1-0	1-0
		Basle	2-3 4-2	6-5
		Atletico Madrid	0-0 0-2	0-2
1974-75	European Cup	Olympiakos	1-1 0-2	1-3

* Billy didn't play

World Club Championship final

At Hampden Park, 18 October 1967.
Celtic (0) 1,   Racing Club (0) 0
McNeill (69)
Celtic: Simpson, Craig, Gemmell, Murdoch, McNeill, Clark, Johnstone, Lennox, Wallace, Auld, Hughes.
Racing Club: Cejas, Perfumo, Dias, Martin, Mori, Basile, Raffo, Rulli, Cardenas, Rodriguez, Maschio.
Referee: J Gardeazabal (Spain).

At Buenos Aires, 1 November 1967.
Racing Club (1) 2,   Celtic (1) 1,
Raffo (33),   Gemmell (22, pen)
Cardenas (48)
Racing Club: Cejas, Perfumo, Chabay, Martin, Rulli, Basile, Raffo, Cardoso, Cardenas, Rodriguez, Maschio.
Celtic: Fallon, Craig, Gemmell, Murdoch, McNeill, Clark, Johnstone, Wallace, Chalmers, O'Neill, Lennox.
Referee: E Marinho (Uruguay).

Play-off at Montevideo, 5 November 1967.
Racing Club (0) 1,   Celtic (0) 0
Cardenas (55)
Celtic: Fallon, Craig, Gemmell, Murdoch, McNeill, Clark, Johnstone, Lennox, Wallace, Auld, Hughes.
Racing Club: Cejas, Perfumo, Chabay, Martin, Rulli, Basile, Cardoso, Maschio, Cardenas, Rodriguez, Raffo.
Referee: R P Osorio (Paraguay).

Appendix Two

GOALSCORING RECORD

Club Games

4 March 1961, League v Ayr United (A).

3 March 1962, League v Dundee (H).

29 September 1962, League v Raith Rovers (A) penalty.

24 April 1965, Scottish Cup final v Dunfermline (Hampden).

3 May 1965, Glasgow Cup v Clyde (H).

17 November 1965, European Cup Winners' Cup v Aarhus (H).

22 August 1966, Glasgow Cup v Rangers (A).

14 September 1966, League Cup v Dunfermline (H).

21 September 1966, League Cup v Dunfermline (A).

8 March 1967, European Cup v Vojvodina (H).

14 October 1967, League v Partick Thistle (A).

18 October 1967, World Club Championship, 1st leg v Racing (Hampden).

24 October 1967, League v Motherwell (H).

16 December 1967, League v Dundee (A).

30 December 1967, League v Dunfermline (H).

3 February 1968, League v Partick Thistle (H).

6 March 1968, League v Aberdeen (H).

19 October 1968, League v St. Johnstone (H).

9 November 1968, League v Arbroath (A).

30 November 1968, League v Hibernian (A).

29 January 1969, Scottish Cup replay v Partick Thistle (H).

22 March 1969, Scottish Cup semi-final v Morton (Hampden).

26 April 1969, Scottish Cup final v Rangers (Hampden).

16 August 1969, League Cup v Raith Rovers (H).

23 August 1969, League Cup v Airdrie (A).
27 December 1969, League v Partick Thistle (H).
17 January 1970, League v Hibernian (A).
25 February 1970, League v Raith Rovers (A).
7 March 1970, League v Dundee United (A) two goals.
16 September 1970, European Cup v Kokkola (H).
23 January 1971, Scottish Cup v Queen of the South (H).
13 March 1971, League v Cowdenbeath (A).
4 September 1971, League v Clyde (H).
27 October 1971, League v Dunfermline (A).
20 November 1971, League v Falkirk (H).
6 May 1972, Scottish Cup final v Hibernian (Hampden).
21 March 1973, Scottish Cup replay v Aberdeen (A).
16 November 1974, League v Airdrie (H).

Country (Full internationals)
13 October 1965, World Cup qualifying tie v Poland (Hampden).
3 May 1969, Home Championship v Wales (Wrexham).
17 May 1969, World Cup qualifying tie v Cyprus (Hampden).

Appendix Three

FULL INTERNATIONAL APPEARANCES

15 April 1961, Home International Championship v England (Wembley) 9-3 defeat.

3 May 1961, World Cup qualifying v Republic of Ireland (Hampden) 4-1 victory.

7 May 1961, World Cup qualifying v Republic of Ireland (Dublin) 3-0 victory.

14 May 1961, World Cup qualifying v Czechoslovakia (Bratislava) 4-0 defeat.

26 September 1961, World Cup qualifying v Czechoslovakia (Hampden) 3-2 victory.

7 October 1961, Home International Championship v Northern Ireland (Belfast) 6-1 victory.

14 April 1962, Home Championship v England (Hampden) 2-0 victory.

2 May 1962, Friendly v Uruguay (Hampden) 3-2 defeat.

9 June 1963, Friendly v Republic of Ireland (Dublin) 1-0 defeat.

13 June 1963, Friendly v Spain (Madrid) 6-2 victory (McNeill at No. 2 position, Ian Ure at Centre-half).

20 November 1963, Home International Championship v Wales (Hampden) 2-1 victory.

11 April 1964, Home International Championship v England (Hampden) 1-0 victory.

12 May 1964, Friendly v West Germany (Hanover) 2-2 draw.

10 April 1965, Home International Championship v England (Wembley) 2-2 draw.

8 May 1965, Friendly v Spain (Hampden) 0-0 draw.

23 May 1965, World Cup qualifying v Poland (Chorzow) 1-1 draw.

27 May 1965, World Cup qualifying v Finland (Helsinki) 2-1 victory.

2 October 1965, Home International Championship v Northern Ireland (Belfast) 3-2 defeat.

13 October 1965, World Cup qualifying v Poland (Hampden) (McNeill – 1 goal) 2-1 defeat.

10 May 1967, Friendly v USSR (Hampden) 2-0 defeat.

24 February 1968, Home International Championship and European Championship qualifying v England (Hampden) (McNeill at No. 4, Ron McKinnon at No. 5) 1-1 draw.

11 December 1968, World Cup qualifying v Cyprus (Nicosia) (McNeill came on as substitute for McKinnon) 5-0 victory.

3 May 1969, Home International Championship v Wales (Wrexham) (McNeill – 1 goal) 5-3 victory.

10 May 1969, Home International Championship v England (Wembley) 4-1 defeat.

17 May 1969, World Cup qualifying v Cyprus (Hampden) (McNeill – 1 goal) 8-0 victory.

22 October 1969, Wold Cup qualifying v West Germany (Hamburg) (McNeill at No. 6, McKinnon at No. 5) 3-2 defeat.

20 May 1972, Home International Championship v Northern Ireland (Hampden) (at Hampden as Scotland refused to play in Belfast) 2-0 victory.

24 May 1972, Home International Championship v Wales (Hampden) 1-0 victory.

27 May 1972, Home International Championship v England (Hampden) 1-0 defeat.

Summary of 29 appearances –
14 victories
10 defeats
 5 draws

Appendix Four

MAJOR CLUB HONOURS

Player

1961 Scottish Cup final v Dunfermline (lost 2-0 in replay).

1963 Scottish Cup final v Rangers (lost 3-0 in replay).

1965 Scottish Cup final v Dunfermline (won 3-2, scored winning goal).

1965 League Cup final v Rangers (won 2-1).

1966 Scottish Cup final v Rangers (lost 1-0 in replay).

1966 League Champions.

1966 League Cup final v Rangers (won 1-0).

1967 Scottish Cup final v Aberdeen (won 2-0).

1967 League Champions.

1967 European Cup final v Inter Milan (won 2-1).

1967 League Cup final v Dundee (won 5-3).

1968 League Champions.

1968 League Cup final v Hibernian (won 6-2).

(Played in Spring 1969, having been postponed from Autumn 1968 due to fire at Hampden).

1969 Scottish Cup final v Rangers (won 4-0, scored one goal).

1969 League Champions.

1969 League Cup final v St. Johnstone (won 1-0).

1970 Scottish Cup final v Aberdeen (lost 3-1).

1970 League Champions.

1970 European Cup final v Feyenoord (lost 2-1 after extra-time).

1970 League Cup final v Rangers (lost 1-0).

1971 Scottish Cup final v Rangers (won 2-1 in replay).

1971 League Champions.

1972 Scottish Cup final v Hibernian (won 6-1, scored one goal).
1972 League Champions.
1972 League Cup final v Hibernian (lost 2-1).
1973 Scottish Cup final v Rangers (lost 3-2).
1973 League Champions.
1973 League Cup final v Dundee (lost 1-0).
1974 Scottish Cup final v Dundee United (won 3-0).
1974 League Champions.
1974 League Cup final v Hibernian (won 6-3).
1975 Scottish Cup final v Airdrie (won 3-1).

Summary	*Wins*	*Losses*
League titles	9	
Scottish Cup	7	5
League Cup	6	3
European Cup	1	1
	23	**9**

Manager

Aberdeen

1978 Scottish Cup final v Rangers (lost 2-1).

Celtic

1979 League Champions.
1980 Scottish Cup final v Rangers (won 1-0 after extra time).
1981 League Champions.
1982 League Champions.
1983 League Cup v Rangers (won 2-1).

Manchester City

1985 Promotion to First Division.

Celtic

1988 League Champions: Scottish Cup final v Dundee United (won 2-1).